MONASTIC WIS

Bernardo Olivera, ocso

Light for My Path

Spiritual Accompaniment

MONASTIC WISDOM SERIES

Patrick Hart, ocso, General Editor

Advisory Board

Michael Casey, ocso
Lawrence S. Cunningham
Bonnie Thurston

Terrence Kardong, osb
Kathleen Norris
Miriam Pollard, ocso

MONASTIC WISDOM SERIES: NUMBER EIGHTEEN

Light for My Path

Spiritual Accompaniment

by

Bernardo Olivera, ocso

Translated by

Augustine Roberts, ocso

Prologue by

Santiago Fidel Ordóñez Fernández, ocso

Cistercian Publications
www.cistercianpublications.org

LITURGICAL PRESS
Collegeville, Minnesota
www.litpress.org

A Cistercian Publications title published by Liturgical Press

Cistercian Publications
Editorial Offices
Abbey of Gethsemani
3642 Monks Road
Trappist, Kentucky 40051
www.cistercianpublications.org

1   2   3   4   5   6   7   8   9

Library of Congress Cataloging-in-Publication Data

Olivera, Bernardo.
    [Luz para mis pasos. English]
    Light for my path : spiritual accompaniment / by Bernardo Olivera ; translated by Augustine Roberts ; prologue by Santiago Fidel Ordóñez Fernández.
        p. cm.
    Includes bibliographical references (p.   ).
    ISBN 978-0-87907-018-2 (pbk.)
    1. Trappists—Spiritual life.   2. Spiritual direction—Christianity. I. Title.

BX4103.O44513   2009
248.8'942—dc22   2008053190

CONTENTS

PROLOGUE

After reading the excellent introduction that Bernardo Olivera himself wrote to the present work, I ask myself what I can add to all he has already said about spiritual accompaniment. He has explained its purpose, the need we have for it, its pastoral importance, its different possible uses, and even his intention of helping us not to waste our time reading about it if we already know what it is, especially if we have practiced it.

Since the purpose of a prologue is basically to motivate readers, that is, to spark our interest so that we read with keener attention and more lasting fruit, I will say something here that could be summed up as follows:

> Spiritual accompaniment is, of itself, a beautiful subject. When we add a good treatment of it by the author, we find ourselves in the presence of a splendid book that has, I believe, a certain charm.
>
> Something charms us when it expresses more than it says—in spite of its relative brevity, this book opens us up to a higher level of awareness. It does so by evoking this higher consciousness and then suggesting that we go there. That is its grace. It is what happens on another level with any gift worth more than its price, such as poetry, where intuition and emotion go beyond the words. It also happens with all the sacraments, the grace of which is in the Grace.

Before developing the two ideas I have mentioned, I wish to inform those who are not aware that our author is Argentine, born in Buenos Aires in 1943, and is the abbot general of the Cistercians of the Strict Observance, commonly known as Trappists. Since his election on September 8, 1990, he is in continual, personal contact with monks, nuns, and communities. Even before that time, he dealt with many persons interested in the search for God. So we have here a work that is the fruit of his experience, his reflection, and his pastoral initiative in presenting for our consideration something as beautiful and as useful as spiritual accompaniment.

THE BEAUTY OF SPIRITUAL ACCOMPANIMENT JUDGED BY THE EXPERIENCE OF THE ONE ACCOMPANIED

The purpose of the present book is to clarify the proper role of the person who is accompanying someone else. When the orientations given here are prudently put into practice, the person being accompanied will enjoy the experience of something along the following lines:

1. It is beautiful to experience that you are really understood by someone, who can be anyone able to do so, and that he or she is sincerely trying to know you. This is chiefly accomplished through a welcoming atmosphere of mutual appreciation, which includes a total, silent, intelligent receptivity. The listener completely forgets self and consciously puts aside the personal impact of whatever you say. There is a silent, yet eloquent, reception of your story, in which you have time to tell all that is really essential. The result is that you exult in the feeling of having been liberated, which comes from expressing yourself freely and completely. It is like holding a big bag of potatoes upside down and having them all fall out. Not a single one is left. But if it is a big bag of flour, more time will be needed. That is, the person who has a richer, more complicated history needs more time to talk. Yet even in that case, the moment comes to finish. A good companion is aware of that and knows how to close the important first session of welcoming receptivity.

2. It is beautiful to see yourself, as in a mirror, from within the person who listens to you. Your image is returned through the

prism of his or her warm welcome. You contrast it with what you would like it to be, and then admit that it is true and accept it with good grace, realism, and even a sense of humor. From that moment on, the truer image becomes yours. You also become simpler, because the one who accompanies you has not become personally involved in your story, but has also focused on what is most important, the essential elements, and has followed the central thread of what has happened. That was what had been difficult to do, perhaps because it hurt or because you wanted somehow to hide it from yourself and not look at it. But your welcoming listener has listened well, has understood what you were asking for, perhaps nonverbally, has seen what you were overlooking and has read it in your emotions, which have come to the surface and been verbalized. Then, with your consent, your listening companion has drawn your attention to a key point, which you dealt with for a longer time. Finally the wonder occurred! You began to give it less importance until you actually let it drop and said goodbye to the very thing that had brought you to this interview of spiritual accompaniment. In the last analysis, the important thing is to discover what you are, in whatever you are living and doing: not how you are living *it*, but how you are living *"yourself,"* that is, what is affecting you so strongly in the surrounding circumstances, and *why* it has such a strong impact on you. Thus you arrive at the heart of the question, or rather at your own heart.

3. It is both beautiful and useful to discover that the ultimate reason why we sometimes "latch on" to certain people or situations is inside us. That is how we grow in self-knowledge, which in turn lets us see how we can solve the problem. Each person has his or her own solution, which normally should not be sought from others. Their help will not profit us if we neither grow nor change, whereas we can and should respond to our own needs from within the global context of our own lives. That is what we are called to out of the depths of our being. When we search for the will of God on this deeper level, we enter into ourselves in order to reply freely and generously from the center of our hearts.

Growth in this response implies seeing it more clearly and carrying it through with courage and patience. Everything then becomes new, which does not mean that it will be easy, but it is now clearly faced and will produce its fruits in due time. It seems to me that the best fruit of spiritual accompaniment is that it requires you to enter into and then come out of yourself in order to move ahead, with your lamp shining bright, to meet the Lord. One's vocation becomes clearer, stronger, and more joyful. We are traveling in the right direction and accompanied from the heart, thanks to an integral spiritual accompaniment.

THE BEAUTY OF SPIRITUAL ACCOMPANIMENT FROM THE VIEWPOINT OF THE ACCOMPANIST

This is where we meet the present book. Its purpose is to help achieve fruitful work as a spiritual companion. It is usually affirmed that there are not many good companions of this kind, at least not ones of the spiritual caliber of Teresa of Avila or Teresa of Calcutta. It could be said that such persons are few and far between, and also especially gifted. Perhaps they themselves benefited from good spiritual accompaniment. There will always be persons who can accompany others in specific circumstances or with certain types of people. In any case, spiritual accompaniment is necessary, since it is part of the service rendered by confessors, superiors, formators, guest house directors, catechists, group moderators, and persons advanced in experience, wisdom, and age. It is also a normal part of all life in Christ, especially in the structural fragmentation of today's technological culture with its oceans of data and information, where each individual thinks of oneself as a self-sufficient unit with unique ideas, when in reality his or her desires are at the mercy of the latest fad or subliminal advertising, which undermine one's deepest convictions.

I have said above that the present book has a certain charm, at least for me. Let me explain.

1. The reader has already seen that the contents are worthy of a scholastic treatise, especially since this book deals with an

initiation to spiritual accompaniment. Throughout the book, however, the author has not remained on the surface. On the contrary, his schematic style is replete with meaning and is charmingly evocative. So we should not expect his work to have the length of an elaborate, patiently written treatise that is still an *initiation* because the field it deals with is becoming increasingly vast. To expect such a treatise would cause a frustrating desire for greater development of the subject matter. Bernardo has done the reverse: he has gone directly to his central purpose and has therefore left to one side the causes of the crisis that exists among some of us, and has avoided—as he puts it—getting involved in the multiplicity of names given to spiritual accompaniment, *or whatever you want to call it.* A pastoral concern for the void to be filled inspires him to offer us some guidelines that are more practical than theoretical.

The charm comes when one becomes aware that throughout the book it is clear that the author is *well read*, that he knows *how to read*, and that his book is well *worth reading*.

> — *He is well read*, which means that he knows what is being written on the subject these days. To realize this, you can look at his table of spiritual accompaniment according to the different tendencies and religious families.

> — *He knows how to read*, that is, he knows how to interiorize what he reads, synthesize it, and then rework it. This process is what lies behind his lists of items, his tables, and his sober, compact style.

> — *He is worth reading.* What he has reworked and presented to us is at the service of those who will read it and can use it for discussion in workshops and study groups, above all within a monastic context.

2. There is also charm in the solidity of his orientation, which is expressed very simply. I would sum up his approach in the following four principles:

NO to any substitute. I say this emphatically: when it comes to accompaniment, no one on earth has been given any power to take the place either of God or of the person being accompanied. Bernardo will say in his very first remark in chapter one that this is a truth that *must never be forgotten.* There is always only one Companion and Guide— the Holy Spirit—whom we are to follow, and we should always remain *a few steps behind.* Moreover, we must *be accompanied* at every step by the person accompanied, in the sense that in him and with him we have to read and interpret God's will in such a way that it is the person being accompanied who answers the Lord. That is why names as sacred as director, guide, counselor, catechist, angel of the church, father, mother, and companion will apply to "spiritual" men and women to the degree that they help people follow the Spirit without taking the Spirit's place by leaning on such "titles" or on a presumed state of grace. One has to have an exquisite sensitivity to know how to disappear when the work has been accomplished and the Other Person, the Spirit, has clearly appeared. However, it is good to remember those names, so as to grow in one's trust in the Lord and ask for the grace to carry out this service well. It is a sign of humble responsibility before God and of transparent moral authority with the person being accompanied. Bernardo insists that we should not be disturbed if the Spirit forgets us, so that the one accompanied can be alone with the Lord. As I see it, it would be a most serious matter if the lack of this sense of responsibility were one of the causes of the crisis of spiritual accompaniment.

NO to confusion, not only concerning roles—as happens when the one accompanying turns into the one accompanied, perhaps due to something he or she shared with the other person—but also concerning duties. This can happen when the person accompanying is strongly influenced in the fulfillment of his or her service as abbot, teacher, professor, or the like, by a lack of confidence on the part of the person being accompanied. There has to be a clear agreement to maintain the trust of the one accompanied and the freedom of the one accompanying. It should also be clarified that what is said by the one accompanied has to be related to the subject of the interview or series of interviews. In this line, the one accompanying should not expect that the one being accompanied tell his or her whole life history, and even less if it is a question of matters of conscience.

YES to complementarity. Spiritual accompaniment has many names. The different ones highlight complementary aspects, which are always present and are interrelated according to changing circumstances. Our author gives preference to the reality of maternity or paternity. It is easy to appreciate how the various names given to this relationship refer to different functions of a father or mother, independently of whether the one exercising it is a man or a woman. This type of complementarity is also important in psychology and psychotherapy, as well as in sacramental confession. The healthy exercise of these two qualities demands respect for their different fields of action and will lead to developing what they have in common.

YES to involvement, which means getting involved, showing a keen interest in the best way to grow in the art of spiritual accompaniment. It is not difficult to become aware of what needs improvement. In fact, this greater skill should be achieved without delay so as to gain new confidence in oneself and greater trust in the Lord, in whose service one wants to be a faithful instrument. In the present book, Bernardo has achieved this goal well, pointing to a new stage of development in which this traditional art will be recovered and used anew. The book is extremely useful and valuable, both for its theoretical principles and, above all, for its practicality. If I praise it here, it is not to embarrass anyone, since the best praise will come from the reader and will be according to the harvest he or she personally reaps from it. And I repeat: the harvest depends on the reader's personal involvement.

Because of that—and to bring this prologue to a close—I mention here what I most remember from the book:

There are plenty of "small" pitfalls. He calls them small because they are lying in wait for everyone, not just for obviously deluded visionaries. They are, however, serious because they are real dangers and are only removed through humility.

In three places he uses the word "fool." What are these three foolish acts? They are: not using spiritual direction ("no one is self-directed, unless one wants to be the disciple of a fool"); letting oneself be seduced by a bad counselor ("only fools . . . mistake his forked tail for a friendly hand"); and hoping to be admitted into a community against the latter's good judgment ("only a fool could think that one can impose his or her own vocation on the community").

In two places he speaks about truths that should not be forgotten, namely, that the Spirit is the only one who accompanies us, and that grace presupposes nature. We always need to keep these principles in mind.

He mentions a particular person who was "accompanied," that is, Brother Michel Fleury of Atlas. Only a few days before his martyrdom, Brother Michel called the spiritual accompaniment he received from his superior, Fr. Christian, "a light for my path." This phrase from the Psalms has inspired the title of the present book and applies it to many lives and to many readers.

* * * *

I also would like to call to mind a person whom all of us would canonize: Teresa of Calcutta. During the process of her beatification, it became known that she had passed through a *dark night*. What none of us imagined was that her night lasted fifty years! Have no doubt about it: if she remained faithful in the darkness we can be sure that she had good spiritual accompaniment. She, too, would have called it "a light for my path."

Santiago Fidel Ordóñez Fernández
Counselor of the Abbot General
Rome, Easter of 2004

INTRODUCTION

Our Brother Michel Fleury, professed monk of the monastery of Our Lady of Atlas, died in Algeria on May 21, 1996. Nine months before, on the feast of the Assumption of the Virgin Mary, and because of the violence rampant throughout the country, he had drawn up his will and testament. There we read the following reflection: "In faith, 'His Word has been a light for my path.'" Michel is clearly referring to the word of God and is quoting verse 115 of Psalm 118, but what is interesting is that he is also referring to the word of his "Superior . . . and brother," that is, Fr. Christian De Chergé, the community's prior.

At this crucial moment of his life, Brother Michel gives us a striking witness of spiritual accompaniment, direction, or guidance, and of what spiritual paternity is.

There are solid reasons to think that spiritual accompaniment—or whatever you might want to call it—is an element that is missing in the lives of many consecrated persons, including monks and nuns. It is not uncommon that many younger members of our communities feel the need for this spiritual service. Sad to say, it seems that the two generations following Vatican II somewhat neglected cultivating this art, which had been so deeply valued by previous generations and is so even now. This is not the time to enter into detail about why this has happened, but simply to point out the need.

The present book is meant to give a modest reply to this need. Its only purpose is to offer some theoretical and practical guidelines to help in initial and permanent monastic formation. I will not waste your time or mine in discussing terminology:

should we say accompaniment, direction, orientation, paternity, or maternity? Although I recognize its limits, my basic choice is the language of accompaniment, referring to the persons involved as accompanying and accompanied. I realize, however, that the language of paternity and maternity has a deeper monastic meaning, and for that reason will use these words too, along with fatherhood and motherhood.

When I speak in a monastic context about the one accompanying, I refer to the person of the abbot or abbess, the novice director and the director of the simply professed, as well as to all those who are at the service of life and accompany it toward the Life, in other words: confessors, guest directors, spiritual brothers, friends, and the like.

It is true that this book is directed to the world of monks and nuns, but it does not stop there. Much of what is going to be said can be applied to the special service of accompaniment given in monastic guesthouses. Besides, the sources of these reflections lie in the great ancient and modern Christian tradition, especially that of the West, and in the contributions of contemporary human sciences. So it will not be uncommon here that we listen to different spiritual teachers and classical humanists, to all of whom we owe a debt of gratitude. In particular we listen to:

> *The great monastic tradition*, which conceives of spiritual help as a charismatic process of giving birth. A relationship is established between a father or mother and a son or daughter in the spirit, yet such an asymmetrical relationship does not block the mutual affection typical of being a son, daughter, father, or mother. The manifestation of conscience, so typical of eremitical desert spirituality, and the fraternal correction practiced among cenobites continue to be, even today, the two pillars of spiritual paternity in the monastic world.

> *Cistercian tradition* as it comes through St. Aelred of Rievaulx. This spiritual heritage establishes a relationship between equals, in which any asymmetry becomes a balanced platform for friendship. The result is mutual accompaniment.

Thoughts and experiences are shared, confronted, clarified, and discerned, either together or alternately, according to circumstances. Saint Teresa of Avila and St. Francis de Sales also experienced this type of spiritual support.

The way of the Carmelites as inspired by Teresa and John of the Cross, and synthesized in the "little way" of Thérèse of Lisieux. The person accompanied has to run the risk of an adventure in love, one that demands deep solitude and a capacity for exposure to the ups and downs of the darkness of faith and lack of support. The one accompanying is eclipsed by this mystery and simply encourages the other to keep going, even at night. The quality of the accompaniment can be judged by one's total submission to the work of the Holy Spirit.

The more proactive Jesuit tradition, in which the person of the spiritual director, while remaining secondary, occupies an important place due to his or her human knowledge and spirit of faith. The person being directed learns as much as possible, but above all exposes his or her situation for the discernment of the director. This asymmetric relationship is emphasized. Any interpersonal affection is not necessarily approved of.

The contribution of the behavioral sciences, especially those with a more existential, person-centered approach. The process here is, above all, the responsibility of the one being accompanied. Even though the relationship is unbalanced, this is greatly tempered by deep respect on the part of the one accompanying and by his or her abstention from any value judgment. We can almost say that the spiritual process is one of accompanied or supervised self-management.

This openness to other traditions should never forget some key features of spiritual accompaniment in a monastic context. It takes place within the normative framework of a rule—in our case that of St. Benedict of Nursia—and cannot exist without wholeheartedly embracing the humble obedience of faith, so typical of the patriarch of the monks of the West. Moreover, the monastic way is slow and repetitive. It calls for large doses of patience and faithfulness on the part of both spiritual father and spiritual son.

On the other hand, the official role of the abbot or abbess as father or mother of the community refers above all to the community as a whole. This means that both abbot and abbess are, in the first place, spiritual accompanists of their respective communities. In the second place, they may perhaps also be such for particular persons. This makes us aware of an important principle, namely that spiritual accompaniment of the monk or nun by the abbot or abbess takes place in a concrete community context.

To develop this last statement, we will have to say something about the abbatial service, even though it goes beyond the strict limits of the theme we are discussing. What is clear, however, is that the abbot and abbess accompany their respective communities spiritually through a type of service to all their brothers and sisters. It is a role that is fatherly, motherly, pastoral, healing, formative, and administrative. In this context of multifaceted service, they also accompany those individual brothers and sisters who freely open their hearts to them in search of light and motivation for believing in the ways of the Spirit and for bringing their lives into deeper conformity to that of the Lord Jesus.

I will conclude this introduction with a piece of advice. This book is simply an introduction to the spiritual accompaniment of individuals. Its purpose is more practical than doctrinal. Those who have received the charism of spiritual fatherhood or motherhood in a more outstanding way will not need any word from me. Those who have received this charism in a more ordinary form can perhaps find something useful here, and those who wish to grow in the art of spiritual accompaniment with the assistance of the Spirit can make use of these pages without feeling that they are wasting their precious time.

1

THE GUIDE AND THE GUIDED

ONLY ONE GUIDE AND ACCOMPANIST

The first thing to bear in mind is that the Holy Spirit is the only Guide and Accompanist. It is something never to forget. The Spirit is the one who, through Christ, carries us to the Father. John of the Cross says it clearly and precisely:

> Directors should reflect that they themselves are not the chief agent, guide, and mover of souls in this matter, but that the principal guide is the Holy Spirit, Who is never neglectful of souls, and that they are instruments for directing them to perfection through faith and the law of God, according to the spirit God gives each one.[1]

This is why the person who takes on the service of accompanist or guide must walk several steps behind the Spirit, so as to be guided by him. The accompanist's main function is to understand the Spirit's action and leadership and to help it as much as possible. Not infrequently it will be necessary to leave the guided person to walk alone, so that the Spirit guides and helps the person directly, without any human intermediary.[2]

---

1. St. John of the Cross, *The Living Flame of Love,* in *Collected Works of St. John of the Cross,* trans. K. Kavanaugh and O. Rodriguez (Washington, DC: ICS Publications, 1964), 3:46.
2. See St. Ignatius of Loyola, *The Spiritual Exercises of St. Ignatius,* trans. L. J. Puhl (Westminster: Newman Press, 1954), 15.

GUIDED BY THE ONE ACCOMPANIED

Being guided by the Spirit is absolutely essential, but there is something more. The accompanist or guide must be guided also by the one he or she is accompanying. This takes place through the latter's openness of heart and sharing of graces and disasters, needs and achievements, difficulties and charisms. Through this humble, sincere presentation of his or her lived experience, the person being guided also becomes a guide for the one doing the accompanying.

The successive sessions of spiritual accompaniment, with the dialogues that such a relationship implies, favor a growth in the intimacy and mutual trust that are the seeds of friendship. Saint Teresa of Avila puts it well: "I would counsel those who practice prayer to seek, at least in the beginning, friendship and association with other persons having the same interest."[3] Saint Francis de Sales agrees:

> Holy Writ says that "a faithful friend is as a strong defense, and he that hath found him hath found a treasure. A faithful friend is the medicine of life and immortality, and they that fear the Lord shall find him."[4] These words (as you may see by the context) regard chiefly our eternal interests, in which above all we require this faithful friend, who will guide our actions by his warning and counsels, . . . let this friendship be at once loving and firm, wholly sacred, divine, spiritual, holy.[5]

In any case, no one is self-directed, unless one wants to be the disciple of a fool. We guide each other and we are all guided by the Holy Spirit. We must never forget that first place is held by the Spirit, and never think that he forgets us. Not only does he not forget us but he also asks for our help and even makes it a requirement. So it would be dangerous to think that our

3. St. Teresa of Avila, *Life*, VII, 20.
4. Sir 6:14-16.
5. St. Francis de Sales, *Introduction to the Devout Life*, 1, 4.

spiritual help, accompaniment, guidance, or friendship might be useless.

NEED FOR ACCOMPANIMENT

Centuries of the church's experience have taught us the need for spiritual accompaniment when we want to reach the heights of holiness. In the first period of Christian spirituality, St. Anthony of the Desert told some monks who were asking him to give them a conference:

> The Scriptures are sufficient for us for instruction, but it is good for us to encourage one another in the faith and to train by means of words. You then, like children, bring what you know to your father and tell him about it while I, because I am your elder in years, will share with you what I know and have accomplished.[6]

We find the same teaching centuries later at the beginning of "Sayings of Light and Love," which were written by John of the Cross to go with his spoken wisdom. These sayings are worth reading and meditating on:

> He who wants to stand alone without the support of a master and guide, will be like the tree that stands alone in a field without a proprietor. No matter how much the tree bears, passers-by will pick the fruit before it ripens . . .

> The virtuous soul that is alone and without a master is like a lone burning coal; it will grow colder rather than hotter.

> He who falls alone remains alone in his fall, and he values his soul little since he entrusts it to himself alone.

> If you do not fear falling alone, how do you presume that you will rise up alone?

> Consider how much more can be accomplished by two together than by one alone.

6. St. Athanasius, *Life of Antony*, 16, 1–2.

He who falls while heavily laden will find it difficult to rise
under the burden.

The blind man who falls will not get up alone in his blind-
ness, and if he does, he will take the wrong road.[7]

John is a poet, but also a theologian who stands taller than his
diminutive physical height. Thus we should not be surprised
that he is able to ground theologically the wise teaching contained in these sayings:

God is so content that the rule and direction of man be
through other men, and that a person be governed by
natural reason, that He definitely does not want us to be-
stow entire credence upon His supernatural communica-
tions, nor be confirmed in their strength and security until
they pass through this human channel of the mouth of man.
As often as He reveals something to a person, He confers
upon that person's soul a kind of inclination to manifest
this to another appropriate person. Until someone does this,
he usually goes without complete satisfaction, for he has
not received it from another man like himself.[8]

Even Pope Leo XIII, himself a pioneer in Catholic social doctrine,
took sides in the discussion in order to dissipate any possible
doubt:

There is no one who calls in question the truth that the Holy
Spirit does work by a secret descent into the souls of the just
and that He stirs them alike by warnings and impulses,
since unless this were the case all outward defense and authority would be unavailing. . . . Moreover, as experience
shows, these monitions and impulses of the Holy Spirit are
for the most part felt through the medium of the aid and
light of an external teaching authority. . . . This, indeed,
belongs to the ordinary law of God's loving providence that

7. John of the Cross, "Sayings of Light and Love," in *Collected Works*, 5 and
7–11.
8. John of the Cross, *Ascent of Mount Carmel*, in *Collected Works*, 2, 22:9.

as He has decreed that men for the most part shall be saved
by the ministry also of men, so has He wished that those
whom He calls to the higher planes of holiness should be
led thereto by men; . . . Such guidance has ever obtained
in the Church; it has been the universal teaching of those
who throughout the ages have been eminent for wisdom
and sanctity, and hence to reject it would be to commit one's
self to a belief at once rash and dangerous.[9]

The unanimous teaching of the saints and the church is clear,
therefore, namely that to climb high you have to do it accompanied by someone else, even though you may walk as if you were
alone. Nevertheless, it must be admitted that in the years after
the Second Vatican Council spiritual "direction" entered a crisis,
though we must also admit that there were reasons justifying the
critics. Today the climate is more peaceful. With the passage of
time, we see a certain lack of health, which we want to remedy.
The church's magisterium is very clear on this point:

> Formation then is a sharing in the *work of the Father* who,
> through the Spirit, fashions the inner attitudes of the Son in
> the hearts of young men and women. Those in charge of
> formation must therefore be very familiar with the path of
> seeking God, so as to be able to *accompany* others on this
> journey. Sensitive to the action of grace, they will also be
> able to point out those obstacles which are less obvious. But
> above all they will disclose the beauty of following Christ
> and the value of the charism by which this is accomplished.
> They will combine the illumination of spiritual wisdom with
> the light shed by *human means*, which can be a help both in
> *discerning the call* and in forming the new man or woman,
> until they are genuinely free. The chief instrument of forma-
> tion is *personal dialogue*, a practice of irreplaceable and com-
> mendable effectiveness which should take place regularly
> and with a certain frequency.[10]

9. Leo XIII, Letter to Cardinal Gibbons, *Testem benevolentiae*, 22.
10. *Vita consecrata*, 66; see n. 64; italics added.

This last text shows how clearly the context and even the language have changed. We are dealing with the action of the Blessed Trinity. Accompaniment takes place thanks to the experience one has acquired and the knowledge of the behavioral sciences, especially the art of personal conversation and dialogue. One no longer speaks of needs, but of a practice that is irreplaceably effective.

The Cistercian's Statute on Formation leaves no doubt on the subject, yet we should recognize that it is still common to experience a vacuum in this regard after the period of initial formation. A simple declaration of principles or an exhortation is not enough to fill it, even though it is better than doing nothing:

> Because they exercise the role of spiritual father or mother of the community, abbots and abbesses have a responsibility to guide their communities towards unity and growth in the Cistercian charism. Through their teaching they develop the identity of the community; through their administration they create the necessary conditions for formation, and through their pastoral care they aim to provide guidance, support and healing for each and every member. They share these responsibilities with all whom they appoint to help them in the service of the community, but more especially with the monks or nuns who accompany those going through the various phases of initial formation. A prolonged and regular spiritual guidance (accompaniment) constitutes an important element of formation, whether initial or ongoing. It leads the monk or the nun towards a real knowledge and acceptance of self, under the eyes of God.[11]

This legislative text clearly states the double dimension in our monasteries of abbatial fatherhood and motherhood. There is the communal dimension, which can never be missing, and the individual dimension, which will depend on the free opening of one's heart.

---

11. Order of Cistercians of the Strict Observance, *Ratio Institutionis*, 15–16.

IDEAL PROFILE OF THE ACCOMPANIST

Let us see if we can sketch the ideal outline or profile of the person doing the accompanying. I say "ideal" on purpose, since it is very difficult to find someone like this in real life, but it will at least help us to know the direction in which we should tend to move.

Christian tradition offers us a fairly good portrait of the spiritual father, guide, master, director, or accompanist. When we consult some well-known masters of the sixteenth and seventeenth centuries, we come up with the following descriptions:

> We should take as guide or father somebody who is both well read and experienced in the things of God.[12]

> It is very important that the master have prudence—I mean that he have good judgment—and experience; if besides these he has learning, so much the better.[13]

> Besides being learned and discreet, a director should have experience.[14]

> He (the spiritual guide and friend) must be filled with charity, knowledge, and discretion.[15]

It is easy to spot the convergence among these different opinions, even though the emphases and accents may vary. The characteristic features of the guide are good judgment, sound teaching, experience both human and divine, prudence, discernment, and charity.

In very few persons do we find all these qualities achieved to perfection. According to John of Avila, they are present in one in a thousand. Francis de Sales is less optimistic and says, "One in ten thousand!" But there is no need to be alarmed. Even in this case, perfection is the enemy of the good. My opinion is that the

---

12. St. John of Avila, *Audi Filia*, 55.
13. Teresa of Avila, *Life*, 13, 16; see also 18–19, and *The Interior Castle*, VI, 3:11.
14. John of the Cross, *Living Flame*, in *Collected Works*, 3:30.
15. Francis de Sales, *Introduction to the Devout Life*, 1:4.

characteristic features of a spiritual companion are present to some degree in ten thousand of every million Christians who live in the spirit of the Gospel and defend their faith.

In a monastic milieu, we can say that the qualities required for being director of novices can also be applied to every monk or nun, including the abbot or abbess, who serves as spiritual companion. These qualities are prudence, faithfulness to the monastic disciplines, ability to communicate and to guide. Perhaps all of this was in St. Benedict's mind when he said somewhat laconically that the novice director should be "gifted in spiritual guidance."[16]

We all realize that it is not the same thing to accompany a novice, a monk or nun in the middle of a vocational crisis, or someone who is well advanced in mystical experience of the divine mystery. One who cannot guide an advanced mystic might be able to handle a novice.

Only for Priests?

In the past, many asked the question of whether spiritual accompaniment should only be given by priests. If this means that the latter have a monopoly on such a service, the answer must be a loud no. But if it is a question of whether such accompaniment is an appropriate part of the priest's pastoral ministry, then the reply is yes. This, however, does not mean that all priests receive such a charism or have the experience necessary for adequate accompaniment. I will return to this subject later, from another point of view. As for the question of whether giving spiritual accompaniment is only for men, the answer has already been given to us by the "ammas" of the Egyptian desert, by such Doctors of the Church as Catherine, Teresa, and Thérèse, and by the lives of several of you who are now reading these pages.

---

16. T. Kardong, *Benedict's Rule: A Translation and Commentary* (Collegeville, MN: Liturgical Press, 1996), 58.6.

SPIRITUAL PARENTHOOD

The cosmos and all living beings have the source of their existence in the fatherhood of God.[17] But in the case of humans there is something special. Human fatherhood and motherhood are unique, being essentially in the likeness of God, who thus is for us both Father and Mother.

Divine Fatherhood and Divine Motherhood

No clarification is needed when we affirm the fatherhood of God. What Jesus has revealed and what is contained in the whole New Testament witnesses to it. But divine motherhood has remained in the shadows through most of Christian tradition. Besides being Father, God is also Mother. Thus the Bible presents him to us as a consoling mother,[18] who lifts her little one up for a kiss, who can never forget the child sprung from her womb,[19] and has a loving, welcoming bosom.[20] Even Jesus compares himself to a broody mother hen gathering her chicks under her wings.[21] This statement of twofold parenthood is of central importance for the theme we are dealing with.

Spiritual accompaniment always implies, to a greater or lesser degree, a sharing in the divine fatherhood in its process of giving birth to sons and daughters, and nurturing them. Every type of spiritual parenthood is thus founded on the parenthood of God. Any spiritual father only works in virtue of sharing in the life of God the Father. His authority is not self-derived but received. It finds its place within the motherly authority or paternity of the church, which is the only way we can fulfill what Jesus says: "Call no one on earth your father; you have but one Father in heaven."[22]

17. See Eph 3:14-16.
18. See Isa 66:13.
19. See Isa 49:15.
20. See Ps 22:10.
21. Luke 13:34.
22. Matt 23:9.

Spiritual Fatherhood

There is a good example in St. Bernard of what this type of parenting implies as the person grows in maturity. It is in Bernard's first letter, written when he was about thirty years old. A certain violence in him still seemed to prevail over mercy. The letter was addressed to his cousin Robert, one of the companions who entered Cîteaux together under Bernard's leadership. A few years later, Robert was one of the twelve founders of Clairvaux and made his profession in the hands of Abbot Bernard. The letter in question was thought to be miraculous, since it was written during a torrential rainfall without getting wet—at least, that is what William of Saint-Thierry states in his early biography of Bernard.[23]

What interests us most here, however, is not any miracle attached to the letter, nor its significance as an apology in favor of the Cistercian way of life as opposed to that of Cluny, nor the story of the young monk Robert, but rather what the letter tells us about its author's approach to our present theme. Over and beyond its value as literature, the letter is revealing. In fact it reveals more transparently, thanks to its high literary quality.

From the beginning to the end of the letter, Bernard says that he is acting from charity. However, it is obvious that many other feelings are involved, such as anger, frustration, sadness, possessiveness, or aggressiveness. Although the severe tone of the letter and its strong military symbolism might denote manly, even paternal, qualities, the idea of fatherhood is not what predominates. Nevertheless, in three key texts from the letter we read:

> Smite thy son with a rod and thou shalt deliver his soul
> from hell. It is where he loves that the Lord bestows
> correction.[24]

---

23. See William of Saint-Thierry, *Vita Prima*, 11:50; also St. Bernard, *Letters*, 32:3.

24. St. Bernard, *Letters*, 1:2, quoting Prov 23:14 and Heb 12:6. See also 1:9, quoting Prov 1:10.

> Having changed yourself, you will find me changed too.
> You may now embrace me without hesitation as a compan-
> ion whom you used to fear as a master.[25]

> See, my son, how I long to lead you now not any more in
> the spirit of slavery to govern you in fear, but in the spirit
> of adoption whereby we cry, "Abba, Father."[26]

This last text is the most important one. Bernard there promises
his own conversion. He promises to be born to what he has not
been, but wants to be. At the same time, he knows very well that
his fatherhood has God the Father as its end. It is a human mediation that will let Robert profess with deep affection and freedom of spirit that God is his Father.

Spiritual Motherhood

Several fathers of the church prolong biblical revelation and
speak of God as Mother. Among them are Clement of Alexandria,
Origen, St. Ireneus of Lyon, St. John Chrysostom, and St. Augustine of Hippo. This maternal concept of God and of Jesus reaches
its high point during the Middle Ages. We could present many
examples of it in the Benedictine-Cistercian tradition. Here is at
least one example, taken from the prayer of St. Anselm, Abbot
of Bec and Archbishop of Canterbury:

> But you, Jesus, Good Master, are you not also a mother? Are
> you not that mother who, like the mother hen, gathers her
> chicks under her wings? Lord, you, too, are a mother, be-
> cause what others have conceived and given birth to, came
> from you. You are the first one who died for them, and by
> dying brought them into the world, so that they in their turn
> could give birth. . . . In fact it is the desire to bring many
> children into life that has made you taste death and through
> your death you have begotten them. You did it by yourself,
> while they do it on your orders, helped by you. You are the

25. Ibid., 1:2. See also 1:3.
26. Ibid., 1:3.

author of life, they are your ministers. So it is you, Lord,
who are the mother.[27]

As you can see, whether it is a question of fatherhood or
motherhood, there is no gift of life unless you embrace death.
One person is born because another dies, but the one who dies
freely is born again. Isn't this what our father and mother, Bernard of Clairvaux, was teaching us a few minutes ago?

It must be stated again that the exercise of spiritual fatherhood goes hand in hand with spiritual motherhood. We can even
say that Bernard seems to be—or wants to be—more *amma* than
abba, more mother than father:

> I have said this, my son, not to put you to shame, but to help
> you as a loving father because if you have many masters in
> Christ, yet you have few fathers. For, if you will allow me
> to say so, I begot you in Religion by word and by example.
> I nourished you with milk when, while yet a child, it was
> all you could take. And I would have given you bread if
> you had waited until you grew up. But alas! How soon and
> how early were you weaned! Now I fear that all I had cher-
> ished with kindness, strengthened with encouragement,
> confirmed with prayers, is even now fading and wasting
> away. Sadly I weep, not for my lost labor, but for the un-
> happy state of my lost child.[28]

Bernard's self-portrait as a mother reaches its extreme when he
identifies himself with the prostitute in the time of King
Solomon:

> My case is the same as that of the harlot Solomon judged,
> whose child was stealthily taken by another who had over-
> lain and killed her own. You too were taken from my side,
> cut from me. My heart cannot forget you, half of it went
> with you, and what remains cannot but suffer.[29]

27. St. Anselm, *Prayers*, 10.
28. St. Bernard, *Letters*, 1:10.
29. Ibid.

The "work" of begetting children is hard. The Abbot of Clairvaux admits it as he prays to the Lord Jesus:

> You know with what agony of heart I waited upon the youth in his trials, how I beat upon your loving ears with my prayers for him, how for his anxieties, troubles, and vexations, I was on fire, and torn, and afflicted. And now, I fear, it has all been in vain.[30]

Actually, Bernard's solicitude was not in vain. Thanks to the good services of Peter the Venerable, young Robert finally returned to Clairvaux, where he lived a holy life. He was sent by Bernard himself to govern the abbey of Maison-Dieu in Besançon. The *Cistercian Menology* recalls his memory on November 29.

And so we see that Bernard, knowing that God is both Father and Mother, lived and interpreted his life-giving service to his monks in a motherly key as well as in a fatherly one. We have just seen it in the letter to Robert written during his first years as abbot, but with time the Abbot of Clairvaux affirmed his convictions even more clearly. For Bernard, everyone fulfilling a ministry of the care of souls should also—and above all—possess motherly qualities such as affection, compassion, tenderness, protection, and nutrition:

> Here is a point for the ear of those superiors who wish always to inspire fear in their communities and rarely promote their welfare. Learn, you who rule the earth. Learn that you must be mothers to those in your care, not masters. Make an effort to arouse the response of love, not that of fear: and should there be occasional need for severity, let it be paternal rather than tyrannical. Show affection as a mother would, correct like a father. Be gentle, avoid harshness, do not resort to blows, expose your breasts: let your bosoms expand with milk, not swell with passion.[31]

---

30. Ibid., 1:7.
31. St. Bernard, *Sermons on the Song of Songs*, 23:2.

Thus St. Bernard becomes identified with a long tradition that unites him to Paul the apostle. Paul thought of himself as father of the community at Corinth, since he "became your father in Christ Jesus through the gospel."[32] But he also saw himself as mother. Both experiences are joined in his first letter to the Thessalonians:

> Although we were able to impose our weight as apostles of Christ . . . we were gentle among you, as a nursing mother cares for her children. With such affection for you, we were determined to share with you not only the gospel of God, but our very selves as well, so dearly beloved had you become to us. . . . As you know, we treated each one of you as a father treats his children, exhorting and encouraging you and insisting that you conduct yourselves as worthy of the God who calls you into his kingdom and glory.[33]

In this quote from Thessalonians we can see the characteristic features of fatherhood: transmission of teaching, stimulation, and reprehension, as well as the maternal qualities of care and tenderness. The result is a fatherly challenge and a motherly welcome.

When Paul wrote to the Christians of Galatia, his "children" whose unfaithful conduct had disappointed and hurt him, he did not hesitate to refer to himself as the most maternal of mothers: "My children, for whom I am again in labor until Christ be formed in you!"[34]

Fatherly and Motherly Attitudes

God is Father and Mother. Thus spiritual accompaniment is a participation in this divine fatherhood and motherhood. It implies attitudes that are both fatherly and motherly because it is an instrument of the grace of a God who is simultaneously Father and Mother.

32. 1 Cor 4:15.
33. 1 Thess 2:7-8, 11-12.
34. Gal 4:19.

Obviously, each person who exercises such accompaniment has his or her graces and limits. Some are more fatherly, others more motherly. The fact of being either man or woman imposes certain conditioning factors, which, however, do not absolutely determine the type of relationship. What really matters here are the natural or acquired dispositions that each person has. But what are the basic dispositions attributed to motherhood or fatherhood in our cultural context? Briefly, they seem to be the following:

— *Motherhood*: an inclination to give, preserve, and promote life; delicate sensitivity; receptivity; and capacity to respond with affection. On the negative or immature side there can be a certain absorbing passivity and a castrating possessiveness.

— *Fatherhood*: an orientation toward initiative and action; capacity for distinguishing and confronting reality. An immature or negative expression of fatherhood is inconsiderate activism or an aloof insensitivity.

We all know spiritual companions of one type or another. Motherly ones are welcoming and understanding, though not so good at clarifying difficulties. Fatherly ones clarify and help us confront the difficulties, but their capacity to understand and accept us could be warmer and more tender.

We know by experience that it is not easy to embody in oneself, in a balanced way, both fatherly and motherly attitudes. But it is possible—even necessary—to acquire a certain complementarity. If the person who accompanies lives a true relationship with the one accompanied, he or she will know how to adapt to the latter's real needs. For example, the accompanying person will have to be more motherly with someone who received little affection in his or her infancy, but with someone who lacked a model of creative, guided action, there will have to be a more fatherly approach.

And we can say, to conclude, that experiential self-knowledge will teach us something strange about ourselves. Although both men and women have been created in the image of God, men do not have a fatherly "instinct" in the same way that women have a motherly one. Many men are not instinctively fatherly and their human nature does not seem to orient them primarily or spontaneously in the direction of fatherhood! In other words, not every man who has children is a father! Was it God who made men like this, or was it sin that disfigured them? It is significant that Adam, after his sin, is not referred to as "father," whereas Eve is "the mother of all the living."[35] Eve will not credit the birth of her first child to Adam, but to God.

We agree that true motherhood is not merely the instinctive one. The maternal dimension appears to be the most complete expression of being a woman. It emphasizes the person as belonging to a particular sex, but without hypersexualizing her. Moreover, it includes both her psychological and her spiritual dimension. Human and personal motherhood assumes the maternal instinct and fulfills it by opening it to other dimensions. That is why true motherly strength communicates life, nurtures it, wants to grow with the other person, encourages the other person to affirm his or her deepest self, believes and hopes that the other will grow better and more completely than she herself will, without expecting gratitude for it. She is stronger than any contradiction or death.

It would seem that spiritual fatherhood in men lacks a natural basis, unless we go to another level and enter into communion with our welcoming, motherly *anima*. Nevertheless, if any man really wants to be a father everything we have said about personal motherhood should also be applied to fatherhood. It is worth asking ourselves whether the motherly instinct of women is an advantage or a hindrance when entering into a relationship of spiritual parenthood. It is a theme that needs deeper discussion.

35. Gen 3:20; see 4:1.

Degrees of Spiritual Parenthood

Objectively speaking and in a sacramental context, we have to say that the only spiritual parent is the person who gives birth to the life of grace in someone else through the sacrament of baptism. In the same way, the priest who administers the sacrament of reconciliation is a spiritual father, since he restores or nourishes the life of grace in someone else.

However, when we speak of spiritual fatherhood we are referring to something over and beyond the nourishment of the life of grace. We are on the level of charisms, not necessarily that of sacraments. In this sense, experience teaches us that spiritual parenthood has different degrees. Here are three of them:

— In the *fullest* sense, spiritual fathers and mothers are those who mediate the life of Christ and teach the way to follow him, offering in their own lives an example to imitate.

— In the *most proper* sense, although it may not be so full as the previous one, we can call spiritual fathers and mothers those who give a determining impulse to the Christian life of others and continue to be a special reference point for their spiritual growth.

— The name of spiritual father or mother can also be applied in a *broad sense* to one whose function consists in accompanying someone or facilitating his or her journey toward Christ, without giving it a decisive orientation.

Although I could seem to contradict myself, I want to add an important truth, namely that the spiritual father or mother in the fullest sense, to the degree that he or she is inspired by the grace of the Spirit and makes the Lord present to us, renews us in the sacramental character of Christian life. That is why the simple presence of a spiritual father or mother is already an instrument communicating life in Christ.

2

PURPOSE AND FUNCTIONS OF
ACCOMPANIMENT

Having looked at the persons involved in spiritual accompaniment, we can now pinpoint better the latter's purpose and functions. We will see, however, that this topic immediately takes us back to the persons involved.

PURPOSE

The purpose of spiritual accompaniment can be expressed in many ways, all of them stating that the fundamental reality involved here is union with God. We can thus say that the purpose of accompaniment consists in helping a person to follow Jesus so as to grow in the life of grace or of the Spirit. We can state this in another way, following the lead of Paul the apostle, by saying that its purpose is to give birth and promote the growth of Christ in the brother or sister.[1]

Since the life of grace grows and the soul is made Christlike through the theological virtues, the latter must be the special object of spiritual accompaniment. Therefore we can say that accompaniment and the dialogue that is its essential component should treat principally the realities of:

— *Faith,* as the gift of responding to and meeting God, and therefore it deals with the life of prayer as a dialogical relationship with God

1. See Gal 4:19 and 1 Cor 4:15.

— *Hope*, that builds the present by seeing the future and pulling us ahead with courageous filial trust

— *Charity*, which unites our desires with the divine desire and grows into multiple forms of service, social interaction, friendship, and solidarity

It seems important to say a word here about loving God in the context of spiritual accompaniment. We often take for granted that we love God. After all, if we serve our neighbor, we love God! This last statement is not false, but we should not forget that God is God. The second commandment of the divine law of charity does not annul the first one! Loving God means recognizing his many gifts and embracing his holy will. It seems very simple, but it requires a serious effort of self-denial in order to reorder our desires and our loves. Saint Bernard's treatise *On Loving God* is an inspiring text in this matter. It can guide both parties involved in spiritual accompaniment.

Accompaniment, then, is a special help to the theological relationship of the monk or nun to God and to neighbor, but the word "special" here does not mean "only" or exclusively. One's theological life is rooted in the life of grace, which sinks its roots into life itself. It is impossible to separate one from the other, unless it is through the death of the life of grace. Life is one in the unity of the person, which is why we can say without any restrictions that the person accompanying journeys with the person accompanied, and accompaniment involves all the aspects of life.

Growth in the life of the Spirit within our hearts usually occurs simultaneously with deep personal integration, which brings our unconscious world into consciousness, even though growth in the Spirit and integration of the unconscious are different realities. Both experiences imply being born again to a new life. Spiritual accompaniment, even though its purpose is to foster the life of grace, does not forget human life itself. Promoting the former usually benefits the latter.

The purpose of spiritual accompaniment, as we have just described it, is intimately related to the name traditionally given to the person who does the accompanying, because giving birth and nurturing life is what makes someone spiritually a father and a mother.

FUNCTIONS

Just as the name "spiritual father" refers to the purpose of accompaniment, so also the other names that are traditionally used point to the functions that the father must fulfill. It is not wrong to say that just as the purpose of anything explains all its functions, likewise the name of father includes all other designations.

Another correlation can also be established, namely that the characteristic features that configure the profile of the accompanist directly refer to that person's functions.

Without wishing to twist reality, I think that the previous two paragraphs can be synthesized as follows:

— Through charity, the *father*, who is also mother and friend, accompanies and helps.

— Thanks to his knowledge as *teacher*, he enlightens and instructs.

— And with his discretion and experience gained as *director*, he advises and guides.

There is still another way to determine the functions of spiritual accompaniment, namely by starting from the situations that the one accompanied will inevitably meet. According to this approach, we would have the following dynamic:

— In the *beginning* and in times of trial: welcome and support

— In *darkness* and times of change: clarification and orientation

— In *setbacks* and falls: confrontation and understanding

— In *projects* and decisions: motivation and confirmation

— In *movements* of the spirit: discernment and space to move

I leave it up to each reader's good judgment to determine which of these functions are more motherly, and which belong more to the father, but in either case if the person accompanying is not simultaneously father and mother, there will be little help given to the one accompanied. Which of these functions are the most important? Without hesitation we can point to the moments of welcome, clarification, confrontation, and discernment. The certainty of this statement is not based on an opinion, but on the simple fact that the four functions just referred to include, in one way or another, all the others. We will see them again, below.

CLARIFICATIONS

Spiritual accompaniment is usually carried out in conjunction with other realities, such as sacramental confession, the abbatial service, or psychotherapy. This fact can often give rise to some special problems. Looking at them more closely will help us, at least indirectly, to understand the functions implied in spiritual accompaniment.

Accompaniment and Confession

Two questions often arise when we speak about this, namely: What are the differences and the similarities between spiritual accompaniment and sacramental reconciliation? And is it better that they occur together or separately? We will have to accept a few general replies to these two questions, replies that have to be nuanced according to whether the accompaniment is taking place in a monastery of monks or in one of nuns, and whether it is during the period of initial formation or later. We only want to add that, in the case of the novice director, the church's experience over the centuries as codified in its laws requires the separation of these two different forms of service. In other words, the director is the one who normally accompanies the novice and

therefore cannot exercise the sacramental ministry of reconciliation in his or her regard.

Differences

We begin with the differences between these two pastoral
ministries. It is clear that the purpose the penitent has in mind
is to confess his or her sins and to receive forgiveness. In contrast,
the one being accompanied is looking for help in spiritual growth.
The purposes are different, but come together in the fact that all
penitents want to grow and all in spiritual accompaniment need
to confess their sins.

In a more detailed synthesis, we can establish clearer distinc-
tions on the basis of the following four questions:

Why? Confession is needed for the forgiveness of mortal
sin and is useful for purifying lesser failings, whereas accompaniment is useful for spiritual growth and is necessary
in particular life situations.

Who? The confessor has to be a minister who has received
the sacrament of sacred orders, but the ministry of accompaniment can be performed by any Christian who has received this charism from God and has sufficient human
knowledge and spiritual experience.

How? Confession must follow a specific liturgical rite as
determined by one of the church's seven sacraments, while
accompaniment is governed by the dynamic of a dialogical
relationship as conditioned by the style and needs of the
persons involved.

When? Devotional confession should take place often, and
as soon as possible when there has been a fall into mortal
sin, without forgetting the many sacramentals, such as holy
water or personal blessings, which can purify recipients
from sins and reconcile us to God and to our brothers and
sisters. Spiritual accompaniment should occur regularly,

following the rhythm decided upon by the two persons involved, keeping in mind the present moment and life situation.

So we can see that there are differences, which explains the practice of the Eastern churches, where the confessor is not the spiritual father. However, these differences are not incompatible, so that in our Western Latin church both ministries often converge in the single person of the priest.

SIMILARITIES

It is worth looking more closely now at the similarities between confession and accompaniment. The same questions we have just used can be our guides.

Both accompaniment and confession converge to form a context of conversion. Why do they both do this? The former exists so that we grow closer to God, the latter so as to separate us from sin. This growth and this separation are the two sides of the single coin of Christian conversion. If we look at who their respective ministers can be, we find a different convergence, this time in the Person of the Holy Spirit: both the accompanist and the confessor are living instruments of forgiveness and of the grace of God's Spirit.

The question of how each type of meeting—the sacramental and the spiritual—develops can also receive a single answer. Both types presuppose a climate of prayer, openness, listening to the Lord, faith, hope, love, and the presence of discernment and good counsel. In fact, the very differences indicated in regard to "when" can easily be converted into a similarity. When? At regular intervals and whenever some particular need arises.

COMBINED OR SEPARATE?

All that we have just said about differences and similarities justifies asking about the suitability of combining or separating accompaniment and confession. Christian tradition supports both possibilities. The differences in the two ministries are the basis of separating them, and the similarities justify combining them. Which is better: to combine them or to separate them?

It is neither easy nor necessary to give an absolute answer, which would exclude the other possibility. In both cases there are reasons for and against. Let us look at some of the more important ones having to do with the present situation in our Latin church.

When accompaniment and confession are *combined*, the sacramental nature of confession places accompaniment in a more explicitly ecclesial context, thus avoiding any type of individualistic intimateness. In the same way, combining them makes it easier to avoid dichotomizing one's theological prayer life from the reality of daily moral living.

Three other advantages could also be pointed out. The discernment more proper to accompaniment can help in examining one's conscience before going to confession with its sacramental absolution. Also, the inner growth that accompaniment reveals more easily can help one not to feel depressed by the presence of sin in his or her life. Moreover, having the confessor as the one accompanying can be more fruitful, because the same person is helping, counseling, judging, and forgiving the person being accompanied, all in the context of a single dialogical encounter.

But let us look now at some reasons for *separating* the two. One reason is easy to guess: if confession and accompaniment are combined, the latter can only be accomplished by celibate men who have been consecrated by the sacrament of the priesthood. In other words, the charism is limited to a particular type of person and if there are already few real accompanists, now there would be very few indeed. In fact, when I say "very few," I am still presupposing that all priests without exception would acquire all they need to exercise the art of accompaniment skillfully.

Added to this is another disadvantage. The combination could lead to confusing, or worse, transforming, accompaniment into a mere moral tactic oriented toward simply not sinning. However, we are not going to organize here a ping-pong game between the pros and the cons to see who wins, because they can both end up winning. So I admit that accompaniment and confession can be either combined or separate. In either case, what is important is that the advantages be exploited and the disadvantages neutralized. But how?

If they go together, the distinction between the two must be maintained so as to avoid confusing one with the other. To achieve this, a few pieces of advice are: first, keep the confession rite intact; second, every meeting for accompaniment should not necessarily include celebrating the sacrament; and third, when one wants to confess a sin and receive absolution for it, he or she should state this intention from the beginning.

When the confessor and the person accompanying are different, it seems important to keep in mind at least the following points: that there should be transparency between the two ministries, with openness to having either one consult the other in some particular situation or refer it to another person according to his or her respective qualifications.

On rereading what I have written in the previous paragraphs on accompaniment and confession, I realize that what is most important is neither separating them nor combining them, but their complementarity.

It is worth adding that the difference between sacramental confession and spiritual accompaniment is especially important in monasteries of nuns. The minister of the sacrament is usually the chaplain or other ordinary or extraordinary confessors, whereas it seems more consistent with the monastic charism that spiritual accompaniment be normally exercised by the abbess, the formation directors, and other older sisters qualified for the ministry. A sign of this is that for admission to profession, the opinion of the sister directors must be listened to, but not the opinion of the confessors.

Accompaniment and the Abbatial Office

We already saw in the introduction to this book that the abbot or abbess is the spiritual accompanist of the community,

but not necessarily of every individual brother or sister. Moreover, the spiritual accompaniment of the individual monk or nun
occurs in the context of a particular community. We can now ask
ourselves something about the advantages and disadvantages
of this arrangement, along with the related questions of whether
there exists any ideal situation and what the real situation is in
the life of our communities.

We begin with the last point, which is the known fact that
abbots and abbesses are not the spiritual fathers or mothers of each
monk or nun of the community. But they are of some of them. Saint
Benedict himself foresees in his Rule that there will be other "spiritual elders"[2] to help the abbot. However, an ideal that becomes
unreal is no longer an ideal in the sense of an end or objective in
view. Therefore we think that the real situation that monastic communities live in is the better and more desirable one.

On the other hand, we should be aware that the purpose of
the abbatial service and that of spiritual accompaniment is one
and the same, namely, conformity to Christ. The abbot or the
abbess will render this service for the community as a whole and
will therefore provide everything necessary so that the monastery
really is "a School for the Lord's service,"[3] a place where the Lord
is sought and found. In this sense, the abbatial office and spiritual
accompaniment are mutually complementary and at the service
of the same goal.

In the case where the abbot or abbess truly exercises spiritual
accompaniment, he or she should follow a few pieces of advice,
which are the fruit of experience. In the first place, they should
not forget that this accompaniment takes place in the context of
a monastic community that lives according to a rule. It would be
very strange if the "disciples" of the abbot or abbess were to have
a special lifestyle, a special *conversatio*. Second, they need to discern very dispassionately whether they should grant any dispen-

2. T. Kardong, *Benedict's Rule: A Translation and Commentary* (Collegeville,
MN: Liturgical Press, 1996), 46.5. Cf. 4.50.

3. Ibid., Prol. 45.

sation from the common life on the basis of their greater knowledge of the Spirit's work in the heart of the brother or sister. Such dispensations might be in reference to the balance between liturgical and personal prayer, or between solitude and living in community. There might also be a question of admitting the monk or nun to profession when there are objective reasons against it that, however, are balanced by the knowledge only coming from something shared in confidence and openness of heart with the superior. A third type of situation can arise when the abbot or abbess have to respect a brother or sister's freedom of spirit and the unique nature of each person's spiritual journey.

If the abbot and abbess do not exercise spiritual accompaniment with particular brothers and sisters, they will have to know how to work with others who do engage in this service. This implies a basic agreement on transparency in particular situations without having such openness damage the necessary confidentiality. Situations such as a possible change of work, sending a member of the community out for advanced studies, or calling a monk to sacred orders show how important such collaboration is. Difficulties often surface and experience proves that moments of obedience in relation to "some heavy or impossible tasks"[4] are never lacking in the lives of those who follow Jesus.

There is much more that could be said on this theme. We conclude by offering three statements, which are open to discussion. An abbot or abbess who totally lacks the grace and practice of spiritual accompaniment runs the risk of reducing his or her service to that of a mere administrator. An abbot or abbess who forgets the community as such, in behalf of accompanying each individual person in particular, runs the risk of destroying the community's common life and any living communion among its members. On the contrary, the abbot or abbess who accompanies some brothers or sisters, while keeping in mind their abbatial service to cenobitic life and working with other spiritual

4. RB 68.1.

accompanists, will avoid many dangers and will be remembered as an exemplary abbot or abbess.

Accompaniment and Psychotherapy

Once again we can establish a relationship here and ask, What is the difference between spiritual accompaniment and psychotherapy, and where do the similarities lie? A complete answer would require more time and space than we have here, so please accept this unfinished beginning of a reply.

We said above that the purpose of spiritual accompaniment is conformity to Christ. Therapy of whatever kind is aimed at good health and personal maturity. So they have different ends in view.

However, this difference of purpose does not prevent a certain mutual relationship between them. In fact, to live a personal relationship with God more freely and in greater depth, a certain personal maturity must be present, although it is also true that conformity to Christ significantly contributes to good health and one's personal maturing process.

A second difference can be stated as follows: the therapist treats persons who suffer in one way or another from some psycho-affective dysfunction, which is why they are called "patients." But the spiritual accompanist usually helps persons who are presumed to be healthy or normal.

Now we all know that the boundary between normality and abnormality is not a clear dividing line between the two. This explains why the accompanist must occasionally take care of basic affective needs—such as the need to belong, to receive recognition, security and the like—that have not been adequately met. Many other times accompanists will have to support, enlighten, and guide the persons they accompany in their normal problems of adaptation or adjustment. For their part, psychologists and therapists can expect to deal with persons with limited mental balance but who live their faith and charity to a heroic degree. Obviously, referring to this lived theological experience can be a key factor in the process of their healing and growth. We are not saying, of course, that the accompanist should disguise himself and play the part of a psychiatrist, nor should the latter act like a spiritual father.

The two differences we have mentioned point to a third one. The formation required and the means employed by one and by the other are necessarily different. It would be a mistake for the spiritual accompanist to help anyone by supplying medication, and a similar statement could be made for the therapist who might pretend to heal or help the growth of his or her patients by means of novenas or vows.

And to close this section, we can add one more difference. The places where the therapist and the accompanist function are different. The former functions in an exclusively human context, whereas the person who accompanies another is doing so in a divine context. Nevertheless, we all know that, except for sin, there is nothing exclusively human or exclusively divine. Both these realities are mutually inclusive and imply each other's existence. There is no spiritual experience that does not rest on what is personal, nor any genuinely human experience that is not open to the spirit and accepts being conditioned by it.

But once again, the differences that we have just pointed out do not prevent a certain amount of convergence. That is to say, it can be very useful to the one who is accompanying if he or she has a theoretical and practical knowledge of psychology, at least enough to be able to detect serious conflicts and refer the person to the corresponding specialist. In this way some ridiculous situations could be avoided, such as when an accompanist only recommends several decades of the rosary in order to help avoid an attack of paranoia, or when, on the contrary, a therapist might try to treat a "passive night of the senses" with nothing more than antidepressants and vitamin C.

In all that we have been saying, what are we driving at? The answer is: a pair of solid convictions. In many circumstances it is absolutely necessary that psychotherapists and those engaged in spiritual accompaniment work together, while obviously observing the confidentiality to which their respective services bind them. And second, insofar as possible, it is very useful that they have a certain acquaintance and training in the discipline that is *not* their specialty. But all this should occur without mixing their skills, nor getting involved in improvised forays into unknown territory. We can be grateful to God that these two convictions are already in practice. In recent years we have witnessed the birth and development of pastoral and religious counseling, integrating many contributions of humanistic psychology, and that of transpersonal psychology, both of which represent a new religious thrust within existential humanistic psychology.

ACCOMPANIMENT AND PSYCHOLOGY

Within the context that we have been describing, it seems useful to say a word about the relation between our life in the Spirit and the dynamics of our psychic makeup, between spiritual theology and the science of psychology. More concretely, it is a question of the relation between spiritual accompaniment and psychology.

There is no doubt that psychology has something to say to spirituality, at least for the following reasons:

> Whatever is received is received according to the mode of the recipient, so we receive divine life according to the dispositions of our personal human life.[5]

> Grace does not destroy our nature, but perfects it, so divine life is infused into our lives as we really live them, using our psychic powers and elevating them at the same time.[6]

However, we should never forget that God is absolutely free to work with his creatures as he sees best. Moreover, no human

---

5. See St. John of the Cross, *The Dark Night,* in *Collected Works of St. John of the Cross,* trans. K. Kavanaugh and O. Rodriguez (Washington, DC: ICS Publications, 1964), 2:10.
6. See St. Thomas Aquinas, *Summa Theologiae,* I, 2, 2, ad. 1.

science can claim for itself the last word on who the human person is and how he or she acts, nor can it pretend to become the supreme norm for measuring the relationship between humans and God. That is why we cannot admit a unilaterally psychological vision of the human mystery, in the sense of reducing man to a conglomerate of psychic energies.[7]

To sum up, what would be the contributions of psychology to spirituality? I would say that there are at least four:

— *To confirm*, from the scientific point of view, the existence and action of factors already acknowledged in ascetic tradition; for example, the existence of different psychological types, and that of higher states of consciousness

— *To make explicit* the facts and principles already present in spirituality as intuitions and generalizations; an example would be the details concerning the defense mechanisms of one's personal ego

— *To explore* new dimensions hardly recognized by spiritual theology, such as the collective unconscious and the presence of archetypes

— *To offer* new contributions that can prevent rash judgments; for example, in some observations of parapsychology in relation to demonic phenomena, or the discoveries in transpersonal psychology concerning higher grades of meditation

We can therefore suspect that spirituality could lose both efficacy and influence in real life if it did not integrate the valid contributions of modern psychology. Similarly, if spirituality puts all its trust in psychological techniques, it would very rapidly pervert its own nature. Ignatius of Loyola expresses this reality in the following way:

7. See Vatican II, *Gaudium et Spes*, 57: "Today's progress in science and technology can foster a certain exclusive emphasis on observable data, and an agnosticism about everything else, since the methods of investigation which these sciences use can be wrongly considered as the supreme rule for seeking the whole truth."

The person who makes God the foundation of all his hope
and conscientiously uses the gifts God has given, both external ones and interior ones, spiritual gifts and bodily gifts,
for the service of his Lord, convinced that God's infinite
strength will accomplish what He wants, either with such
instruments or without them, but also convinced that his
own conscientious effort is pleasing to God when it is made,
as it should, for His love, this person, I say, is not bending
his knee to Baal, but to God, whom he is acknowledging as
Author not only of grace, but also of nature.[8]

All the above helps us understand, too, that psychology can
render a valuable service to spiritual accompaniment. Indeed,
the four major schools of contemporary psychology offer us some
very useful elements to work with. We can present their contributions synthetically as follows:

Schools:	Psycho-dynamic	Behavioral	Humanistic	Existential
Authors:	Freud, Jung, Adler . . .	Watson, Shinner, Eysench . . .	Maslow, Rogers, Fromm . . .	Frankl, May, Boss . . .
Problems:	Unconscious conflicts	Inadequate reactions to stimuli	Assertiveness and negative self-image	Search for meaning, existential frustration
Usefulness:	Defense mechanisms and personality types	Exercise of virtues and removal of vices	Non-directive counseling centered on the client	Vocational work and ministry to the sick

8. Letter to Juan Álvarez, Aug. 18, 1549.

3

WELCOMING, SPEAKING, DISCERNING

Much of what has been said so far has been somewhat theoretical, even though oriented to practice. So the present section will deal with practice as the embodiment of theory. In other words, we will try to show how the functions of an accompanist are translated into the dialogical session of spiritual accompaniment.

All of this presupposes that the accompanist is convinced of the following truth: namely, that the author of inner transformation is the Holy Spirit, with the immediate collaboration of the person being accompanied and the secondary, subordinate help of any other mediation, including that of the accompanist.

We have already seen the four prime functions that the accompanist has to fulfill in his or her service of spiritual accompaniment. These functions can also be understood as different moments or aspects of the dialogical relationship. Not all of them will be active in every particular session, but they are necessary in the process as a whole. In some sense, when they are taken as a group, these functions let us create a model for the art of accompaniment. They are: welcome, clarification, confrontation, and discernment.

Still more is involved. Even when a formal relationship of spiritual accompaniment is not established, these four functions are, by themselves, extremely useful in any type of interpersonal relationship, such as that of the abbot or abbess with the members of the community, the give and take of daily community life, the

relation of the guest master to a guest passing several days of
retreat in the guesthouse, or the relation of a discerning portress
to a person asking for advice.

WELCOMING

When we speak of welcoming someone we usually imply
an affectionate element at the first moment of a relationship.
Without denying such a reality, the context of spiritual accompaniment requires that we add other components, namely: authenticity, acceptance, listening, understanding, and empathy.
These five realities are the ingredients that make up the welcome.
Let's look at them one by one.

Authenticity

Authenticity in its full sense is the coherence between what
you *are*, what you *want*, what you *think*, what you *feel*, what you
say, and what you *do*. Thus understood, authenticity is the equivalent of having personal integrity. So when we say that someone
is authentic, we are saying that he or she is "a real person," "guile-
less," "himself" or "herself."

We can also say that being authentic is a form of love. It
fosters total self-donation, in which one gives what is most genuinely personal, not dividing oneself and then acting out of a non-
existent fiction. Like personal integrity and love, authenticity
requires effort and exercise. Above all it implies self-knowledge
and self-acceptance:

> *Self-knowledge*: of one's own usual habits of thinking, feel-
> ing, and doing—both the positive habits and the negative
> ones
>
> *Self-acceptance*: so as to live interiorly in peace and freedom,
> without having to be on the defensive, consciously or un-
> consciously protecting one's weak points

In relation to the welcome necessary for spiritual dialogue, we can say that the accompanist welcomes, above all, by being authentic, genuine, and thus showing who he or she really is. In this context it is particularly necessary that authenticity be in reference to what each person says and feels, especially to what one feels, and this on two levels:

> On the *intra*personal level, the accompanist lets the feelings experienced in the relationship come into conscious awareness and accepts them as his or her own.

> On the *inter*personal level, the accompanist is free to communicate his or her own feelings or not to communicate them, but always in a constructive way.

Of course, when it is a question of communicating negative feelings continually experienced during the dialogical encounter in a way that will be helpful for the person being accompanied, several conditions have to be borne in mind, at least these two:

> — The relational process of accompaniment should have advanced enough so that a certain trust exists, which will permit communication and guarantee its acceptance.

> — The feeling should be expressed in a totally subjective way as coming entirely from oneself, avoiding any accusation of the person being accompanied or any imposition of guilt on that person, as if he or she were the cause of the accompanist's feelings.

The authenticity of the accompanist will always produce good fruit, of which the chief ones—and those most easy to observe—are these: a climate of freedom and trust, inner freedom of the person accompanied, a stimulus for the other person to be authentic, and space for the action of the Spirit of truth who sets us free.

On the contrary, the lack of authenticity creates a climate of ambiguity, due above all to the double language—one verbal, the other nonverbal—that enters into the dialogue. This confu-

sion eventually causes the accompanied person to become inse-
cure and to lose confidence in the accompanist.

If we want to grow in authenticity as spiritual accompanists,
we first have to be authentic in all the circumstances of our lives,
then learn to recognize the feelings that move us, identify them
precisely, and call them by their real names. Finally, we will have
to revise our lives and evaluate the sweet and bitter fruits produced by the communication or noncommunication of our feelings in previous meetings and dialogues.

When I spoke once about this topic, someone asked, Is it
good, or not so good, that the accompanist reveal his or her self
by communicating opinions, experiences, or doubts about sub-
jects of daily life? Generally, when there is a climate of intimacy
or a friendly relationship, one's authenticity leads to self-revela-
tion. Several prudent recommendations should be kept in mind
if this self-disclosure is going to be positive and useful for the
person being accompanied:

— There should be a climate of mutual trust created by close,
   ongoing contacts.

— One should be morally certain that it will be useful for
   the growth of the accompanied person in the concrete
   situation in which he or she is living.

— The accompanist must renounce all desire of self-gratifi-
   cation in this revelation of self.

— Keep silent in front of persons who will misinterpret what
   is shared, either through their immaturity or because of
   the formation they have received.

Because of what we have just said about authenticity as a
quality of welcoming, the following conclusion becomes clear:
welcoming is much more a question of being than of doing. We
welcome someone by what we are, not by what we do.

Acceptance

We pass now to acceptance as a constitutive part of the act of welcome in the context of a spiritual dialogue. A clarification must first be made in order to avoid a common misunderstanding. Acceptance is not synonymous with approval. We are always bound to accept our neighbors, but we do not always have to approve of their behavior or their misdeeds. At the beginning, accepting other people can include the global, implicit acceptance of their mistaken conduct, but that is only a starting point that is open to growth and presupposes their sincere desire to grow.

Let us look for a moment at Jesus, since we find in him an incomparable model of acceptance of our neighbor. In the house of Simon, he welcomed and accepted the prostitute who anointed his feet. He knew that she was capable of much love but did not praise her sins. Instead, he forgave them.[1] He did the same with the woman caught in adultery. When they brought her to him for his judgment, he did not condemn her but simply told her not to sin anymore.[2] He accepted Judas and his treacherous kiss, and with his acceptance invited him to conversion.[3] He accepted those who crucified him and even asked pardon for them, for they were acting out of ignorance.[4] He also accepted and welcomed the good thief, not because of his robberies but because he had repented of them.[5] And the gospels offer us many other examples of how this acceptance converted hearts. It is enough to think of how Jesus accepted his disciple Peter.

In the dialogical session of spiritual accompaniment, the accompanist must accept the one accompanied with every sign of respect, interest, appreciation, and affection, just as that person is, without the idea that he or she "should be like me." One must accept the other in his or her personal originality and respect that

1. See Luke 7:36-50.
2. See John 8:1-11.
3. See Luke 22:47-48.
4. See Luke 23:33-34.
5. See Luke 23:39-43.

person as a sacred minister, as a walking freedom that wants and is capable of originality and fullness of life. Such acceptation is a form of that love that is not rude and does not seek its own interests but simply receives with affection.

Accepting the other person always produces good fruits that, even though they may not be many, are very useful. In the first place, acceptance reduces anxiety, minimizes the drama of certain situations, calms the spirit, and lets people enter their interior world. Moreover, the experience of being respectfully accepted reduces personal frustration and the risk of self-rejection, letting self-acceptance grow along with a healthy confidence in oneself. All of this increases the capacity to make responsible decisions. It commits the person to continued growth and to overcoming the obstacles that might arise.

What would be the main signs of a low level of acceptance in one's welcoming attitude? The most evident, frightening—and common!—signs are the following:

— Giving rapid orders, hasty advice, or moralizing exhortations and offering ready-made solutions needing very little personal adjustment

— Judging or labeling, asking more than a single short question, or changing the theme of the dialogue or steering it in a preconceived direction

— Underestimating the significance of shared confidences, lessening the importance of what the person being accompanied thinks is vital, or showing scant interest in it

If we want to grow in acceptance—and if we do not want to, we might as well resign as spiritual accompanists—we can often ask ourselves, Do I show respect for persons and for their freedom? Do I pay attention to their feelings and ideas? Do I communicate interest and appreciation for what they are and do? Do I let them express themselves and speak as much as they want? Do I show my faith in their real possibilities and capacities for growth?

Actually, the simplest way to evaluate our acceptance and our respect is to ask ourselves how good we are at listening, but this means that we are already shifting to another component of the welcoming process.

Listening

The third component of a good welcome, intimately connected to the previous one and even more so with the next one, is the act of listening. To listen is much more than merely to hear, and in the context of spiritual dialogue it is more important than speaking. It is not for nothing that we have two ears but only one mouth, which means that we are meant to listen twice as much as to speak.

It is impossible to put into a single, narrow word the full meaning of what it is to listen. Those who have listened well— Jesus among them—teach us by their words and their lives that to listen is:

— *To shut up*, in order to start hearing, which is obvious but often forgotten

— *To keep silent*, so as to be recollected, attentive, and centered on the other person

— *To respect* the other precisely as other

— *To let the other speak*, open up the self, describe situations, search for solutions

— *To feel* what the other person feels

— *To be aware* of one's own feelings, but without breaking the flow of communication

— *To observe* postures, gestures, and behavior

— *To remember* faithfully what was said so as to bring it up later

— *Not to influence* the other, even by gestures or attitudes

— *Not to substitute* one's own experience for that of the other person

— *Not to generalize*, thus disembodying the other's lived experience

— *Not to discriminate* between what is important and what is banal

All these features of good listening are important. Nevertheless, I am going to emphasize two of them: to keep silent and to observe.

KEEPING SILENT

The first thing required for keeping silent is to shut up. Not speaking lets the inner world become silent and calm, that is, it stops thinking. And it is precisely this interior silence that lets the accompanist sincerely welcome both the words and the inner being of the person accompanied.

When it is present at the right moment, this silence is deeply fruitful. First it produces the repose needed for the accompanied person to continue. Then it allows more time for the person to focus and process all his or her experience, integrate his or her feelings, and think about what to say. But when the accompanist does not say anything, simply because he or she does not know what to say or is unable to do so, the fruits are unsubstantial, even bitter.

It seems to me that the capital sins against silence and listening—that is to say, the principal causes that make them difficult—can be reduced to the following three:

— We take for granted that people expect solutions to their problems.

— We prepare our replies at the same time that we listen, that is, if we are listening.

— We listen to what affects us or interests us, and hardly even hear the rest.

Nonverbal Observation and Communication

To observe, you have to pay attention. And not just to words but also to gestures, bodily postures, and behavior. This nonverbal language, which is almost always involuntary or unconscious, is often more expressive—and actually more authentic—than many words.

The gamut of what can be observed in the other party extends to the whole person. Without pretending a complete list, we can at least pinpoint the following personal dimensions:

— *Physical Aspect*: bodily composure, life energy, gestures, movements, tone of voice, type of clothes, personal hygiene

— *Affective Aspect*: emotional state; intensity of feelings; free expression of feelings or their repression; degree of coherence between feelings and words, and between feelings and gestures

— *Intellectual Aspect*: capacity to understand and assimilate, precision in the use of words, logical discourse, appeal to principles and ideas

— *Volitional Aspect*: ability to make decisions, firmness of character, daydreaming, imposition of opinions

— *Relational Aspect*: interest for meetings and dialogue, confidence in self and in others, withdrawal from others, aggressiveness, defensiveness, dependence, indifference, disdain

If we pay attention to nonverbal communication, we will understand much that is not communicated by words, which can be because the person does not want to, or is not able to, or simply does not know how to. Yet he or she will transmit many messages to us by means of:

— The *Glance*: communicating understanding, inquiry, sadness, joy, rejection, surprise, complicity

— The *Mouth*: transmitting surprise, anger, complacency, doubt, disdain, seduction

— The *Skin*: its blush speaks of shame or inhibition, its paleness of fear, its moistness of nervousness or anxiety

— The *Voice*: its tone and its changes express a gamut of feelings and moods

— The *Bodily Postures*: shrugging can reveal self-protection, crossed arms or legs can show a closed attitude, relaxation can be a gauge of trust, stiffness can denote control, leaning forward can show interest or intimacy

John of the Cross tells us that "individuals whose spirit is purified can naturally perceive—some more than others—the inclinations and talents of men and what lies in the heart or interior spirit. They derive this knowledge through exterior indications (even though extremely slight) such as words, gestures, and other signs."[6] However, in this matter it is very important not to jump to hasty conclusions. This is the recommendation not only of saints and psychologists, but also of prudence and common sense.

And be careful! As accompanists we, too, send out a lot of nonverbal messages. We have to become aware of them and use them for the good of the other person. It would be shameful if our words said yes, and our gestures communicated no.

Perhaps some might consider all this emphasis on nonverbal language as slightly exaggerated. There is a simple way of showing its importance, namely, engaging in a conversation and, in the middle of it, continue talking with our eyes closed. Then we can ask ourselves, When did we listen more and better: when we used only our ears or when we had both ears and eyes functioning? Listening does not occur in the same manner during a telephone conversation as it does face-to-face.

6. St. John of the Cross, *The Ascent of Mount Carmel*, in *Collected Works of St. John of the Cross*, trans. K. Kavanaugh and O. Rodriguez (Washington, DC: ICS Publications, 1964), 2, 26:14.

Recent studies on communication strongly emphasize nonverbal communication: tone of voice, eye movements, facial expressions, body movements and posture, and distancing and the use of space. Paradoxically, nonverbal language is more eloquent than speech. It may seem to be an exaggeration, but they say that 38 percent of our communication comes across through tone of voice, with another 55 percent through other bodily expressions, leaving only 7 percent due to verbal communication.

Attentive listening transmits to the accompanied person a feeling of being accepted and understood. It encourages the person to continue speaking and prepares him or her to listen, since only after having spoken and expressed oneself will the person be able to listen and pay attention to what we can say. Listening occupies the central place in welcoming the other person. It opens the door to the gift of self, makes it possible to show oneself sincerely, and lets someone come in, be present, and stay. Without such listening, it is impossible to understand the one we are accompanying, or help the person understand his or her own self.

Understanding

If we want to understand our neighbors in ordinary life, we will have to begin by making the following truths our own:

— We are not necessarily equals. (What I like may not be what she likes; what I am thinking is probably not what he is thinking.)

— External behavior is not always a faithful reflection of interior feelings. (She became impatient with me not because she hates me, but because she is depressed and feels frustrated from working in the kitchen for so many years.)

— Any personal problem can seldom be reduced to a simple, single cause. (Besides being sensitive to "titles," he feels largely disliked from not having succeeded as novice director.)

— Our neighbors appreciate it when we pay attention to them, but without forcing them into our mold. ("Call me whenever you want to and we can meet immediately. It will be a real joy to hear what you have to say.")

— Understanding has its limits. ("How am I going to understand everything about you if I am a mystery to myself?")

— To understand one's neighbor is to help that person in self-understanding.

Presupposing these truths, we can now treat of understanding in the specific context of spiritual accompaniment. In such a context, understanding is the capacity to put oneself in the place of the other person, yet without ceasing to be oneself. In other words, it is to perceive and feel interior and exterior reality just as the accompanied person perceives and feels it. When I speak of perceiving, I am referring to the world of experience as our field of perception and frame of reference.

Obviously, to enter into the world of the accompanied person, the accompanist must leave his or her own world, yet without becoming identified with that of the other person. But what does the accompanied person's experiential world consist of? It will be difficult to enter into it if we do not know what it is. Perhaps it will help if we point out the different aspects of that world, at least the following ones:

The *objective* world that the accompanied person confronts. This consists of persons, things, happenings, and circumstances that exist outside the person or even without the person having anything to do with them.

The *subjective* world composed of:

— things *perceived*—everything that the accompanied person consciously sees and accepts, thinks, understands, interprets, verbalizes, and communicates about the objective world that he or she has encountered or is encountering

— things *emphasized*—everything perceived that attracts the attention of the person and concentrates his or her experience, since it is compatible with their self-image

— things *deformed*—everything that the person's defense mechanisms, especially the unconscious ones, filter, modify, reinterpret or wrongly interpret concerning the objective world of personal experience

— things *rejected*—everything not consciously perceived, because it goes against one's personal ego, normal experience, self-concept, or for other reasons

— things *resonated*—all affective resonance that confrontational encounters have produced, as well as the present state of one's feelings

This very simple analysis of the world of experience lets us draw some conclusions that are not without their importance. First, the objective world is wider than what is simply perceived. Also, what is perceived is, in turn, usually greater than what is emphasized, but is not always greater that what is deformed or rejected. And finally, what resonates interiorly is coextensive with one's entire subjective world.

Where are these conclusions leading us? They point to this: if we want to understand the persons we are accompanying and help them to understand themselves, then . . .

— Our understanding of the *objective* world that they have encountered has to be as adequate and certain as possible. That is the only way that we will be able to help them objectify their subjective experiences.

— What we perceive of their *subjective* world has to be broader than what they themselves perceive, which means that it has to include what they deform and reject. That is how we will be able to help them broaden what they have perceived.

— What we *emphasize* should be everything that we perceive, about them, for if we do not de-emphasize our own experience, we will not be able to enter into theirs.

— What we *deform* or *reject* must be reduced to a minimum. Unless it is, we will become blind guides leading other blind persons.

— Our affective *resonance* will try to be on the same wavelength as the affective resonance they themselves are experiencing. Unless it is, we will not understand what is most their own in their experiences, which is the subjective element.

From all this, we can see that it is not easy to understand others. Leaving one's own experiential world to enter that of someone else is not an easy task. The principal causes of this difficulty seem to be: *egocentrism*, which measures the other with the yardstick of our own experience; mental *rigidity*; personal *insecurities*; the tendency to be *judgmental*; and an indulgence in an *authoritarian* style of giving orders. One more cause can be added: affective *immaturity*, which translates into an attitude of either distant indifference or excessive emotional identification. It is not at all easy to find the right distance to maintain in accompanying and helping someone without abandoning, substituting for, or confusing that person.

Empathy

Nevertheless, listening and understanding are not only intellectual processes but also affective ones, and this is where empathy enters the scene. Empathy is the harmoniously shared vibration of feelings and lived experiences, the predominantly affective and experiential understanding of someone else's affective life.

Thus empathy is the master key that unlocks the experiential world of the person we are accompanying. Through it, we understand what someone else is living and feeling, and thus are able to help that person's self-understanding. It is more than mere sympathy, which is only an affectionate mode of understanding that belongs to the senses, but does not necessarily enter into the other person's experiential world. In empathy, however, the experience of affectionate understanding is enriched by the help of the imagination, intellectual insight, and the vast possibilities of unconscious intuitions.

Empathetic listening presupposes affectivity centered in the other person and motivated by the free gift of self to one's neighbor. At the same time, however, empathy requires a real capacity for openness and welcome of the other precisely as other. Naturally speaking, this type of relationship is lived more spontaneously by a woman than by a man. It is she who shows more interest in the other's personal, intimate life and is more receptive, respectful, and sensitive to another person's confidences. Feminine affectivity is rich in its double orientation to welcoming and giving, to being loved and loving. This sensitivity predisposes the woman to welcome and to understand more deeply those who open their hearts to her. All other circumstances being equal, we have to say that a woman is more mature than a man for welcoming without dominating and for guiding without directing. This is doubtless part of the "genius of women" that lets them see what is human in both men and other women—"in their greatness and limitations; they try to go out to them and help them."[7] A woman is aware "that God entrusts the human being to her in a special way" and that "this in a particular way determines their vocation."[8]

To a greater or lesser degree, we all have the capacity for empathy. Generally speaking, good teachers, convincing salespersons, and heads of corporations who know how to work with their subordinates have a high degree of empathy. Each one of us, without being aware of it, exercises empathy many times during the day. We do it, for example, while reading a fascinating book, when watching some moving story or show, by actively

7. John Paul II, *Letter to Women*, 12.
8. John Paul II, *Mulieris Dignitatem*, 30.

participating in a well prepared Easter or Christmas liturgy. Any artistic experience is highly empathetic. In fact, empathetic understanding can occur in any interesting conversation, above all with persons whom we love.

If it is true that leaving one's own world is a prerequisite for understanding someone else's point of view, then it has to be said that empathetic understanding totally depends on this type of exit and entrance. The person who does not relax, give up, and let go will never experience empathy in the way I am describing it here. There is no empathy without welcome, and no welcome without empathy. What is the key to empathetic understanding? Love intertwined with knowledge.

To put it briefly, when the spiritual accompanist is authentic, he or she accepts, listens, understands, and empathizes. It is then that the accompanied person feels and knows, without a shadow of a doubt, what it means to be welcomed.

AFFECTIVITY

We are going to take advantage of the present context to say something more about the role of affectivity in welcoming and in the general relationship of spiritual accompaniment. The first thing to say is that affectivity is always present. When we spoke of listening, we were saying that the accompanist should try to feel what the accompanied person is feeling, as a necessary condition for understanding that person. We mentioned listening in relation to acceptance, saying that someone who accepts another with affection makes the acceptance felt.

Accepting someone affectionately is the equivalent of accepting that person with a love that makes itself felt, but that is very far from any kind of fatherhood, motherhood, protectiveness, or pretended trust. The right kind of affectionate acceptance is always effective, because it goes out to meet and answer two basic needs of every human being, namely, appreciation and love. When these needs are answered, the fruits are trust in oneself and self-assurance.

Mistakes in this area can be on the side of either defect or excess. In the former case, there can be distancing, indifference, or, even worse, coldness. The fruits such defects produce are feelings of abandonment or insecurity, little encouragement to grow, and, in the long run, bringing the spiritual accompaniment itself to an end.

On the other hand, excessive affection in the relationship can also produce bitter fruit. The most common one is affective dependency. The loss of the necessary prudent distance will also give rise to a personal involvement and identification that will prevent any type of objectivity. In the end, the mutual affection can cause the initial appreciation to pass from empathy to a love affair, which is a very complex and different phenomenon from what was initially intended.

Now we are going to present in more detail some affective phenomena that can become present in the dialogue of a spiritual meeting, namely, reciprocity, interference, transference, and countertransference.

Reciprocity: Here we have the normal, natural mutual affection and esteem present in every interpersonal relation. There is no question of an exclusive affection, but rather of one that can be multiplied in other similar relationships, each one maintaining its own particular characteristics.

Interference: Along with such a reciprocal, affectionate relationship, there can also be other affective factors that interfere in it. These can have different causes, for example, the association with affections typical of other reciprocal relationships, such as the relation with one's spouse, the reliving of other similar situations in the past, or the insufficient resolution of past conflicts. What is important is that the relationship at hand be the primary one, despite the disturbing effect of these interferences. Otherwise, prudence would advise suspending or breaking off the relationship.

Transference: This is a phenomenon that has been thoroughly studied by depth psychology. It is a strong, almost constant,

unconscious mechanism consisting of the projection onto
the accompanist of the qualities of significant people in the
life of the person being accompanied. The result is that the
one accompanied feels and acts as if the accompanist is the
cause of his or her feelings. The most typical cases of this
are usually when the person sees the accompanist as:

— An intransigent *superior*, against whom you have to defend yourself

— An accusing *judge*, in whose presence you have to justify
yourself

— An all-powerful *benefactor*, whom you must keep happy
so that he or she can help you

— A *professional*, who will solve all your problems without
charge

— Someone who can *decide things* for you and thus free you
from all responsibility

— Someone *full of wisdom*, who never makes a mistake and
in whom you can have total confidence

There are three typical attitudes that reveal the presence of
transference in the person being accompanied. There can
be *stubbornness* in some attitudes, topics, or problems; *re-
sistance* to proposals or suggestions; and *mixed feelings* concerning the accompanist.

This transference on the part of the one accompanied can
sometimes help at the beginning, for example, by affording
a deeper knowledge of the accompanied person, thanks to
seeing how he or she lives the present under the influence
of the past. But if the accompaniment is going to last beyond
the initial phases, the relationship will have to be redirected
toward what is the real situation. In general, the bond created by transference is broken when it becomes the explicit
subject of the conversation.

Countertransference: This is the inappropriate response of the accompanist to transference received, that is, the transference of his or her own affective feelings onto the person being accompanied. It can occur during a temporary situation of fatigue or stress produced at the end of a hard day, or it can be a question of a defensive projection when one's weak side is exposed or provoked. The most typical case is often caused by mutual affective involvement due to an indiscreet lowering of the necessary professional distance. The existence of this type of countertransference can be detected by questions such as: Am I looking forward to the visit of the person I am accompanying? Am I fed up with him? Do I feel like throwing the person out or, the other extreme, wanting to protect her? A sincere reply to these questions can be enough to untangle or resolve the situation.

But what is the right balance in the affective component of a spiritual meeting or dialogue? To tell the truth, there are so many variable factors that it is impossible to establish a general rule that would apply to all cases. The task of the spiritual accompanist is to discern in each case the quality and intensity of affection in the relationship. To do this, the accompanist has to take into account not only moral values, but also circumstances such as age, gender, sensitivity, personal maturity, formation received, mutual trust, emotional state at the time, and the topic being discussed. By their fruits you will know them!

From all we have said, it is easy to see the need of a certain degree of affective maturity if a person is going to be a really helpful spiritual accompanist. Although it is a simplification, we can say that this maturity consists in a coherent harmony between affectivity and rationality, the latter term including both intelligence and will. Maturity creates a context of freedom for loving with a spontaneous spirit of self-offering. It is a dynamic reality in a continual growth process. A normal degree of affective maturity is needed in order to:

— Promote and accompany this growth with one's own personal life
— Support peacefully and cheerfully the ups and downs of the accompanied person
— Communicate positive, constructive affection without getting overly enmeshed in it

The failures in spiritual accompaniment can often be traced to weaknesses in the spiritual accompanist. And the precise lack is the necessary degree of affective maturity. This matter would deserve a detailed treatment, since it is the root of many failures.

CLARIFYING

Let us now look at the second basic function of the accompanist in the process of spiritual accompaniment, namely that of clarification. To clarify, in this context, means above all to become a mirror, so that the accompanied person can see the faithful reflection of his or her reality. The simplest practical means to achieve this reflection is by reformulation, and we will add a word about replacement and the description of possibilities.

Reformulation

Reformulation is to put into words, as clearly as possible, what the accompanist has understood from the person accompanied. It can be done in several ways, which give rise to the various types of reformulation:

Reiteration refers to the simple repetition of what was understood. It is usually best to introduce the repetition by phrases like, "You say that . . .", but it can also be reduced to simple gestures of assent or the repetition of the final words of a sentence.

Clarification is where the accompanist reflects elements that have not been fully formulated, but that easily follow from what has been said. It is important here to avoid giving any impression of being like a detective, so one must show the greatest respect and an infinite delicacy. This can be done by introducing the clarification with words that are more subjective, such as, "Excuse me, if I understand correctly, you are saying that . . ."

Imaging Feelings is mirroring the emotional state of the person being accompanied, along with everything that is not the objective content of the communication, in other words, all that has been nonverbally communicated. This reflection of the feelings of the other person must be clear and easily understood. It can be reduced to a simple question, such as, "How are you feeling?", followed by a reiteration: "I have the feeling that you are a little . . ." Everything we said above about observation and nonverbal communication is very useful for this type of rephrasing.

Resuming is useful, above all, if the accompanied person has spoken for a long stretch of time. It helps to sum up the main ideas, or at least the ones most easily perceived as such.

Reformulating well reduces the distance between the accompanist and the person accompanied. It lets the latter become aware of being understood, while the former checks to be sure that he or she is really accompanying.

Replacement

Another basic element in clarification consists of placing the present situation of the accompanied person back into the total life context of both the person and those with whom he or she lives and works. This technique of replacement permits the one accompanied to gradually take a healthy distance from his or her personal situation and to see it more clearly as it is, both in itself and in reference to its possible causes and effects. The best fruit of a well formulated replacement is the gradual acceptance of reality just as it is.

Possibilities

If the circumstances require it, the accompanist can describe the possibilities more explicitly. However, one has to be very careful that these possibilities are already in the heart of the one being accompanied, even though only implicitly. Sometimes they are evident to everyone except that very person. Different tools can be used to achieve this passage from what is implicit to what is clear:

— *Questions* can be asked that respect the person's freedom: "Have you thought that . . . ?"

— *Information* can be given that is brief and timely: "I know that there are now . . ."

— Simple *advice* can be given, with some subjective aspect: "It seems to me that it is better to . . ."

— A *warning* can be given, mixed with a motivation: "I'm surprised that someone like you would want to . . ."

As a conclusion to the present section, it seems important to add that the function of the accompanist within this context of clarification is that of helping someone else. It is the responsibility of the accompanied person to gradually objectify his or her situation with concepts. This, of course, will never be done totally or even adequately, but it is a necessary step for coming to understand, appropriate, and integrate the situation into one's whole life.

CONFRONTING

In this case, the accompanist not only replies to the accompanied person but goes a step ahead and invites the person to confront his or her own personal reality with what the gospel requires, with the special obligations of the monastic state, or with decisions made by the community.

In his letter to the Christians of Ephesus, St. Paul offers us a very useful piece of advice that is applicable here, namely, that we should be "living the truth in love."[9] The dialogues of Jesus with the Samaritan woman and with the adulteress are two splendid examples of confrontation with the truth in one's own life, thanks to a context of welcoming love.[10]

In One's Own Life

Confrontation is, above all, the unmasking of one's own life, getting rid of all disguises, becoming aware of one's own little lies, and then assuming personal responsibility for them. The simplest ways of confrontation, from among many others, are the following:

— Point out the *contradiction* between two statements: "I don't understand it. Last week you said that you were attracted to monastic life, and now you say that you are going to enter a seminary, even though you don't like priests."

— Show the *ambiguity* between theory and practice: "You say that prayer is an important part of your life, but it seems as if you spend very little time at it each day."

— Refer to the *consequences* that follow from something already known and accepted: "I don't see how you can want to be a part of the *schola* if you know that the condition of your larynx won't let you sing every day."

Sooner or later, especially at the beginning of monastic life, this confrontation will also have to deal with the vices that undermine the search for God. A practical, concrete way of doing this is to suggest reading, and then dialoguing on, some classic texts about this subject, such as:

The eight capital vices according to John Cassian, in his *Institutes*, 5–12

9. Eph 4:15.
10. See John 4:4-42; 8:1-11.

The twelve degrees of pride according to St. Bernard, in his treatise *On Humility and Pride*, 28–56

The seven imperfections of beginners according to St. John of the Cross, *The Dark Night*, 1, 2–14

Confrontation with one's own life and, even more, receiving help toward making this confrontation is no easy matter. Any confrontation engaged in by an accompanist needs to combine the following characteristics if it is going to bear fruit:

— Its only purpose must be the growth of the accompanied person.

— It must be made in a climate of respect, understanding, and empathy.

— Any hint of aggressiveness must be avoided.

— The accompanist must search for and find the best moment for it.

— There must be enough receptive capacity and openness on the part of the person being accompanied.

— The confrontation should refer more to the person's way of acting than to his or her way of being.

In the Gospel

Christian values and the demands of the Gospel should never be put between parentheses, but rather be progressively presented so that one's life is gradually confronted with the invitations of the Good News. This is how the accompanist becomes a servant of God's word. The fact of letting this Word take flesh in one's own life invites the brother or sister to let it grow in his or her life. Such a confrontation with the truth of the Gospel can be made in the form of suggestions. Jesus himself did this through, for instance:

— Affirmative suggestions: "If you want to . . . go . . . sell . . ."

— Questions that make the person think: "Why were you looking for me?"

— Suggestions inviting the person to come to a decision: "If you knew the gift of God and who is saying to you . . ."

— Abstract suggestions that open the listener up to making them personal in their own life: "No one can enter the kingdom of God without being born of water and Spirit."

— Wordless suggestions through action: "He walked ahead of them going up to Jerusalem."

Another practical way to achieve personal confrontation with the Gospel is to suggest special biblical texts for the person to confront during the time of daily *lectio*.

In Monastic Life

Saint Benedict bases himself on experience when he recommends that the newcomer to monastic life read the Rule three times before being admitted into the community. In this way the candidate clearly "knows what he is getting into."[11] In other words, nobody enters, remains, or dies in the cenobium without having been confronted many times with what has to be done if one wants to be a monk or a nun. And of course, if you do not do this on your own initiative, others will see that it happens.

What we have just said about the Rule can also be applied in some way to the Order's constitutions and to local traditions, decisions, and agreements. Visitations are usually the normal way to exercise such confrontation. The old "chapter of faults" had the same purpose, although its spirit was different. In any case, no one can persevere in communal life without continually confronting and adjusting to the "form" of the community.

11. T. Kardong, *Benedict's Rule: A Translation and Commentary* (Collegeville, MN: Liturgical Press, 1996), 58.12.

Revision of Life

The Gospel's invitations and demands, the duties belonging to the monastic state of life, the decisions of the community: all these can be the object of communal confrontation. It is true that no one wants to go back to the old observance of the "chapter of faults." However, it is also true that confrontation on a community level has an efficacy that is irreplaceable. Being convinced of this, I here offer a few guidelines for what could be a community's "revision of life" on behalf of all concerned.

The basis for such a revision lies in the faith conviction that the Lord fulfills his promise to be in the midst of those who "are gathered together in my name."[12] It is precisely this presence of the Lord that is the motive for renewing our life of communion and our union with him. That is why the members want—in the best gospel sense of the phrase—to "win over" their brother or sister.[13]

It is basically a question of reviewing community life on the level of being and of doing, either in a general way or in a particular aspect. It is in this context that each one's self-correction and/or correction of neighbor is both possible and desirable. Obviously this correction refers to what can realistically be corrected and what harms the common good.

There are several possible ways to proceed, or methods to follow. In our day there is the classical method of "seeing, judging, and acting." In detail, this implies:

> *Seeing*: An event, a topic, or a norm in the rule or constitutions is chosen and made the object of dialogue, discussing how it is lived in the community at the present moment.
>
> *Judging*: The causes and effects of communal and personal life are judged in their relation to the chosen topic. This includes the attitudes of the group or of individuals concerning the topic. If necessary, personal clarifications can be made, but without becoming any form of self-defense. If anyone

12. Matt 18:20.
13. See Matt 18:15.

has anything to say about someone else, it should be done by placing what is negative into a positive context.

Acting: The session finishes with a sincere, concrete commitment to grow as a community and as persons. If there is need for forgiveness, this should be asked for and given.

To sum up, we all know that personal or communal confrontation is not easy, for many reasons. We have to overcome, above all, the fear of possible anger on the part of the person being accompanied. In the second place, it is much more pleasant to be positive and considerate. Thus it is easier to say to a brother, "There is still a half bottle of wine left," than to say, "Why did you drink a whole half bottle of wine?" And finally, no one likes to inflict suffering, even when it is a condition for further growth. Yet a genuine spiritual accompanist cannot neglect this essential part of the process.

DISCERNING

We are here at the most important and crucial moment of spiritual accompaniment. Discernment is needed because of the twofold condition of Christian life. In the first place, we have to admit that we are influenced by spiritual beings, namely, God and the demons. Secondly, we also have to admit that neither the content of the faith nor the way toward life is immediately evident to us. Without discernment we cannot lead an authentically Christian life nor walk in the way of truth.

Now, when we speak of spiritual discernment, we use the word "spiritual" as an adjective qualifying—that is, indicating the quality of—discernment. Our discerning will be spiritual in the measure of our incorporation into Christ and the inspiration of the Spirit: "No one knows what pertains to God except the Spirit of God. . . . Now the natural person does not accept what pertains to the Spirit of God, . . . because it is judged spiritually."[14] It is only by a transformation of our worldly mentality

14. 1 Cor 2:11, 14.

into the new Christian mentality, that of Christ himself, that we can "discern what is the will of God, what is good and pleasing and perfect."[15]

On the other hand, when we speak of discernment of spirits, the "of spirits" refers to the immediate object of discernment, that is, interior movements or lights, the interior spiritual influence of different types of phenomena. Here, in the context of spiritual accompaniment and to be precise, we are speaking of discernment as "the spiritual discernment of spirits."

For our present purposes and not wanting to repeat ourselves, we will try to clarify some points concerning the nature, object, and criteria of discernment. Then we will provide a few clarifications that seem to be important.

What Is Discernment?

Terminology

Before getting wrapped up in our subject, it seems best to say a few words about the vocabulary of discernment. This will help us to understand its nature. Our word "discernment," which has only been used for the last three centuries, is the translation of the Greek *diácrisis*. This is the same word that St. Paul uses in his first letter to the Corinthians when he lists the charisms and includes among them the "discernment of spirits."[16] But first it will be helpful to look at some texts in Greek that treat of Christian asceticism.

In Greek

Continuing the terminology of St. Paul, *St. Anthony of the Desert*, who was admirable "for the grace given [him] by the Lord for the discernment of spirits,"[17] tells us:

15. Rom 12:2.
16. 1 Cor 12:10.
17. St. Athanasius, *Life of Antony*, 44.

We need great ascetic discipline and great prayer so that each person may receive through the Holy Spirit the gift of discerning spirits and will be able to understand which of them are less evil and which are the evil ones, and what kind of activity each of them is busy with and how to defeat each one and cast it out.[18]

The first Greek life of *St. Pachomius*, founder of cenobitism, speaks of his "discernment of spirits" in relation to the appearance of a demon who pretended to pass himself off as Christ. Pachomius unmasked him by applying a simple criterion of distinction.[19]

Starting in the fifth century, the phrase becomes rarely used, or rather it begins to be supplanted by the concept of "discernment of passionate thoughts (*logismoi*)," or just "discernment" without any other specification. It is not easy to say with certainty what the reasons for this change were, but it seems that as the spirits to be discerned were depersonalized and supplanted by the capital sins, the classical phrase was changed. We can look at some examples of this new situation.

In the extremely interesting collection of letters of Abba *Barsanuphius of Gaza*, we find the following counsel: "You should have a particular moment in the morning or in the evening, for discerning passionate thoughts."[20]

We find another eloquent example of this transformation and domestication in Bishop *Diádocus of Photiké* and his *Hundred Chapters on Spiritual Perfection*. It is impossible for me to make a four-line summary of the rich teaching contained in his chapters 26–35, 36–40, and 75–89. Diádocus does not speak of the discernment of spirits, but of discernment pure and simple. He specifies that "the meaning present in the mind is a precise taste of what one discerns,"[21] and distinguishes two types of consolation by making a keen analysis of them.[22]

18. Ibid., 22. See the whole discourse, nn. 16–43.
19. St. Pachomius, *Life of Pachomius*, 87.
20. Barsanuphius, *Correspondence*, 395; see 265.
21. Diádocus, *Hundred Chapters on Spiritual Perfection*, 30.
22. Ibid., 31–33.

John Climacus, abbot of Mount Sinai, is also a witness to the evolution. In his famous *Spiritual Ladder*, he teaches that "from obedience is born humility, from humility comes discernment . . . discernment begets clear thinking."[23] But what is discernment for Climacus?

> Among beginners, discernment consists in true self-knowledge. Among proficients, it is a spiritual sense which flawlessly distinguishes what is truly good from what is only naturally so, or from what is contrary to it. Among the perfect, it is a knowledge that comes from a divine enlightenment, and that can shed its light on what is obscure for others. Or perhaps in a more general way, discernment is, by definition, the sure perception of God's will in all occasions, in all places and in all circumstances. It is only found among those who are pure of heart, pure of body and pure in the mouth.[24]

As can be seen, Christian literature in Greek considers discernment as a gift to win and to receive. It distinguishes different degrees of discernment and is especially concerned with good and evil spirits and interior movements.

In Latin

The history of the word "discernment" is slightly more complex in the writings of Latin authors, whether they are patristic or monastic ones.

The second conference of *John Cassian*, which he puts into the mouth of Abbot Moses, treats of the virtue of discretion (*discretio*). At the beginning of the conference, Cassian quotes St. Paul and says that the discernment of spirits "is not an insignificant gift, nor an earthly one, but rather a great gift of divine grace."[25] In the course of Moses' discourse, the spirits disappear from the

---

23. Climacus, *Spiritual Ladder*, 4:1115.
24. Ibid., 26:1; see also 173.
25. Cassian, *Conferences*, 2:1.

scene and discernment becomes that discretion that consists in "walking on the royal road of the just mean, and is the mother, the guardian and the moderator of all the virtues."[26]

The Rule of *St. Benedict* offers a very rich teaching on discretion, although a simple reading is not enough to discover its depth. The abbot is described as someone who "should give prudent and moderate orders (*discernat et temperet*)"[27] so as to be able to act with "discretion."[28] And this discretion is, for both Benedict and the preceding monastic tradition, "the mother of virtues."[29] Saint Benedict and his Rule are remarkable because of their discretion, as St. Gregory the Great states in relation to the Rule, which itself is "outstanding for its discretion."[30] In other words, Benedict has the grace and art of both recognizing and discerning spirits and human affairs, good and evil, what is fitting or unfitting according to the circumstances of time and place. He also possesses in a high degree the graces of moderation, circumspection, measuredness, deliberation: in a word, prudence.

In the work of Pope *Gregory the Great*, the word "discretion" appears often, referring both to discernment and to moderation. I will only quote one text, which is full of a certain joyful gravity. It refers to our nostrils as symbols of the art of distinguishing with moderation between good and evil:

> Someone with too small a nose will be unable to keep the measure of discretion. This is because we distinguish by our nose between perfumes and bad odors. Thus discretion, thanks to which we choose virtues and reject crimes, is rightly expressed by one's nose. That is why Scripture, when it sings the praise of the Spouse, says, "Your nose is like the tower on Lebanon."[31] This is because Holy Church truly watches with attention and discretion, what trials will come for her from

26. Ibid., 2:4.
27. RB 64.17-19.
28. Ibid.
29. Ibid.
30. St. Gregory the Great, *Dialogues*, 2:36.
31. Song 7:5.

different events, foreseeing from afar the future attacks of the vices. However, there are persons who, because they do not want to appear to be stupid, stray onto the wrong path due to their extreme subtleness. Such persons engage in endless investigations beyond the measure of reason. That is why Scripture mentions the man with a "long aquiline nose."[32] The nose that is long or aquiline is actually symbolic of an excessive subtlety in discretion that departs from healthy moderation and strays away from right judgment in its actions.[33]

We can place medieval monastic writers in this same context, since they follow the same line of thought. The best example among them all is *St. Bernard of Clairvaux*. We can look at a few of his texts, which will serve as examples. We use for our guide that discrete moderation that the Rule speaks of when it says, *"ne quid nimis."* Don't overdo it![34]

Now as for those who have attained to this grace of devotion, there is, as I think, one more danger lying in their way. They need to be on their guard against "the scourge that lays waste at noon."[35] For Satan himself, as the Apostle tells us, "masquerades as an angel of light."[36] This is a danger to be feared by such as discharge all their duties with sensible devotion: following their attraction, they may injure their health by indiscreet austerities, and thus be obliged—not without much spiritual loss—to occupy themselves with the care of a weakened body. Consequently he who would run without danger of falling must be enlightened by the day of discretion, which is the mother of virtues and the crown of perfection, for by discretion we are taught to avoid excess in everything. This is the eighth day in which the child is circumcised, for discretion truly circumcises, by keeping us between the extremes of too much and too little.[37]

32. See Lev 21:17.
33. St. Gregory the Great, *Pastoral Rule*, 1:11.
34. RB 64.12.
35. Ps 91:6.
36. 2 Cor 11:14.
37. St. Bernard, *Circumcision*, 3:11.

Discretion permits moderation, but also, unfortunately, mediocrity, lukewarmness, and self-complacency, which can hide under the cloak of discretion. "Such discretion disgraces real discretion. . . . It is not discretion but disorder."[38] Bernard draws a radical conclusion from this situation, saying that "since such perfection is a very rare bird (*rara ista avis*) on earth, let obedience stand to you, my brethren, in place of discretion, so that you shall do nothing more, nothing less, nothing otherwise than has been commanded."[39] On the other hand, those who govern others cannot be satisfied with just being discreet, because "without the fervor of charity the virtue of discretion is lifeless, and intense fervor goes headlong without the curb of discretion. Praiseworthy the man then who possesses them both: the fervor that enlivens discretion, the discretion that regulates fervor."[40]

Discretion is also discernment. The Holy Spirit bestows this gift on those who only search for peace and always keep their purity of intention. Bernard hastens to say that there are very few such persons:

> For who can keep watch over his inward thoughts so closely and so assiduously, whether they merely occur to him or whether he is their author, as to be able to decide clearly which of the heart's illicit desires are the fruit of his own frailty, which an insinuation of the devil? I believe this is more than mortals can achieve, unless by the light of the Holy Spirit they receive that special gift which the Apostle lists with the other charisms under the name of *discernment of spirits*.[41]

The purpose of this discernment is the dedicated search for God and for his will. This dedication is given by the Holy Spirit. "It is he who probes the depth of our hearts, he who discerns the thoughts and intentions of the heart (*discretor cogitationum et intentionum cordis*).[42] He does not allow the slightest amount of

38. St. Bernard, *Apología*, 16–17.
39. St. Bernard, *Circumcision*, 3:11.
40. St. Bernard, *On the Song*, 23:8.
41. Ibid., 32:6. See also Sermon 33.
42. Heb 4:12.

chaff to settle inside the dwelling of a heart which he possesses, but consumes it in an instant with a fire of the most minute inspection. He is the sweet and gentle Spirit who bends our will, or rather straightens and directs it more fully toward his own so that we may be able to understand his will truly, love it fervently, and fulfill it effectually."[43]

To sum up, we can easily see that in Latin literature dealing with the spiritual life, the word "discretion" translates two different, complementary realities: discernment and its resulting moderation, or correct measure. We should keep in mind that the Latin verb *cernere* has two meanings. One is "to separate," the other is "to see." This twofold meaning is present in the act of discerning: seeing in order to separate, then to act well, that is, with measure and moderation. Scholastic writers of the thirteenth century distinguished these two aspects more radically. With them, *seeing* became identified with the cardinal virtue of prudence.[44]

In Ignatius of Loyola

What we have just seen will help us understand the wealth of teaching contained in the "Rules for the Discernment of Spirits," which *St. Ignatius of Loyola* drew up "for understanding to some extent the different movements produced in the soul and for recognizing those that are good, to admit them, and those that are bad, to reject them."[45] It is St. Ignatius, writing to St. Francis Borgia about the reforming pseudo-mysticism of two members of the Society of Jesus, who best synthesizes the most significant meaning of the preceding tradition:

> It is most fitting and very necessary to discern and examine these spirits. God our Lord gives a special grace for this because of its supreme importance. It is a grace of discretion

43. St. Bernard, *Pentecost*, 2:8. See also *Various Sermons*, 23.

44. See St. Thomas Aquinas, *Summa Theologiae*, II, 64, 4.

45. St. Ignatius of Loyola, *The Spiritual Exercises of St. Ignatius*, trans. L. J. Puhl (Westminster: Newman Press, 1954), 313.

of spirits *gratia data*—given gratuitously—to his servants, as the Apostle says, a grace of aid, which must be exercised with human effort, especially with prudence and good doctrine.[46]

Conclusions

In conclusion, what does this overview of Greek and Latin terms teach us? We can sum it up by saying that the word *discretio* (discretion) translates two Greek words: *diácrisis* (discernment) and *metrón* (measure). Discretion is, therefore:

— The ability to distinguish or discern the origin and orientation of the *movements* that spring up within us

— And the ability to walk in the royal road of right measure, the *just mean*, as a result of having exercised the above capacity to discern

Therefore, when we speak with precision about a discreet person, we are referring to someone who possesses discernment and balance. This is exactly what John of the Cross means when he requires any spiritual director to be *discreet*, besides being wise and experienced.[47]

Having clarified the meaning of the words, it is now a question of investigating the reality itself. Actually, our understanding of the terminology has already given us an initial answer to the question on the nature of discernment, but we continue with a briefer, yet more precise, analysis.

THE NATURE OF DISCERNMENT

To understand what discernment is, we should keep in mind the following basic *principle*, which we can express in the words of the discreet doctor:

46. *Letter* of July 1549.
47. See St. John of the Cross, *The Living Flame of Love*, in *Collected Works*, 3:30.

> I presuppose that there are three kinds of thoughts in my
> mind, namely: one which is strictly my own and arises
> wholly from my own free will; then two others which come
> from without, the one from the good spirit, and the other
> from the evil one.[48]

In our daily life we are especially interested in distinguishing the
orientation of the inner movements we experience—thoughts,
intentions, desires, intuitions, feelings—so we can say that there
are two types of movements: one good, moving us toward what
is good, the other bad, moving us toward evil.[49] Also note that
when we say bad or evil, we are referring as well to what is less
good or to what is only apparently a greater good. With these
premises clear, we can give an initial response to the question of
the *nature* of discernment.

Discernment is, above all, a *sublime charism* that should be
received with gratitude and consolation, because it is both adequate and useful for the needs of the church. However, it should
not be prayed for recklessly, nor should we presume that we will
receive from it the results that should be the fruit of our own
spiritual labor.[50]

Discernment is a supernatural instinct of the spirit that is
prophetic in nature and lets the receiver intuitively perceive the
salvific or malicious origin and thrust of desires, thoughts, and
other interior movements. These can be either one's own inner
movements or someone else's. Discerning implies accepting the
possibility of subjective error due to wrong interpretations or
bad use of the supernatural light received.[51]

Without denying anything we have just stated, we should
add that almost always, when we speak of discernment, we are
dealing with a *common charism* to be received and worked for. As

48. St. Ignatius, *Spiritual Exercises*, 32. See Cassian, *Conferences*, 1:19-20.

49. See St. Bernard, *Various Sermons*, 23.

50. See Vatican II, *Lumen Gentium*, 12.

51. See St. Ignatius, *Letter* 51 of July 1549, and *Letter* 75 of June 5, 1552, both
to St. Francis Borgia.

the *New Penitential Ritual* says, "Discernment of spirits is the intimate knowledge of God's work in the heart of men, a gift of the Holy Spirit and fruit of charity."[52] More than just having us see the origin of the movements stirred up by different causes, this charism lets us:

— *Feel*, or become aware of, the movements that stir up inside us

— *Distinguish* or interpret their good or bad nature according to their orientation toward what is good or what is evil

— *Determine* the discreet behavior required by these inner movements

It is, therefore, a gift acquired through the exercise of charity, prudence, and experience in applying the criteria of discernment of spirits. In other words, discernment is a prudent contemplative judgment, oriented to action, on our interior religious life as a channel and place where divine grace acts.

By discernment we share in the Father's vision of reality and we unite ourselves to his saving will, which guides human hearts and human history toward himself through the free cooperation of human beings with the action of the Holy Spirit.

Discernment is a type of knowledge that is practical, rather than theoretical or speculative. We can say that it is knowledge in faith, ordered to putting love into action and thus embodying here and now what we hope to receive in its fullness, namely, the loving will of the Father. Since it is a question of a charism that is both sublime and common, discernment is always for the good of the church.[53] Thus it would not make sense to practice it on the fringes of the church.

52. *Ritual*, 3.10a. See Phil 1:8-10.
53. See 1 Cor 12:7.

What Do You Discern?

What is the *object* of the act of discernment? We have already said in different ways that the purpose or object of discernment is the will of God in a concrete situation. In particular, the object of discernment is the entire spiritual life, even life as such, judged from within the vision of faith. That is why St. Paul can say, "Test everything; retain what is good."[54] We can also say that the purpose of discernment is the same as that of spiritual accompaniment, namely, conformity to Christ in the Spirit.

Now the exercise of this gift, this art, throughout the history of Christian spirituality teaches us that its immediate object consists of two classes of interior phenomena that come from different causes, namely:

— Interior lights and movements, which determine the direction of important life decisions

— Spiritual consolations and desolations, which produce either peace or a spiritual struggle

From another point of view, and in more general terms, we would also include one's usual spirit, one's spontaneous, stable tendency, as an object of discernment. In fact, this type of discernment takes place even before discerning the passing movements of the moment. At the same time, it is a result of discerning them over a long period of time. In the same way, growth crises in prayer or in one's ministry, and especially vocational attractions or possible changes of one's state of life, are also objects of discernment.

It seems useful to quote here some words of St. Francis de Sales, which overflow with common sense:

> I must warn you, Theotimus, against a troublesome temptation that sometimes comes to souls who have a great desire to follow in all things what best accords with God's will. On every occasion the enemy puts them in doubt as to whether it is God's will for them to do one thing rather than

54. 1 Thess 5:21.

another. For example, they ask whether it is God's will for them to dine with a certain friend or not to dine with him, whether they should wear gray clothes or black, whether they should fast on Friday or Saturday, whether they should take some recreation or abstain from it. In this way they waste a great deal of time. While busying and perplexing themselves to discover what is better, they needlessly lose opportunities to do many good deeds. The accomplishment of such deeds would be more to God's glory than this distinction between the good and the better with which they have amused themselves could ever be. It is not common practice to weigh small coins but only pieces of value. . . . In like manner, we do not have to weigh all kinds of little actions to learn if some have greater value than others. . . . It is not giving good service to a master to spend as much time thinking about what is to be done as in doing what is required. We should measure out our attention according to the importance of what we undertake.[55]

And finally, let us say that in this work of discernment, the person being accompanied must interpret and judge his or her own situation. The accompanist helps the one accompanied by making use of theoretical and practical knowledge, spiritual experience, and the advantages gained from not being the person directly "in the soup." It is always true that "nobody is a good judge of one's own case," even though the judgment of one's own conscience has the next to the last word. In any case, we need to listen to St. Bernard saying, "He becomes the disciple of a fool who sets up to be his own teacher,"[56] and "Anyone who avoids giving his confidence to his director will find he is giving it to a seducer."[57]

How Do You Discern?

The purpose of discernment is to embrace the Father's will, but how does he make his will clear? How do we know it? In the

55. St. Francis de Sales, *On the Love of God*, 8:14.
56. St. Bernard, *Letters*, 87:7 (90:7 in the B.S. James edition).
57. St. Bernard, *On the Song*, 77:6.

first place, we need to realize clearly that God's will is shown to us by what are called *criteria*, which are different ways his will is known. They include:

— *Commands and prohibitions* revealed by God directly or through the church and its legitimate authorities

— *Right reason*, created in us by God as a reflection of his own divine intelligence

— *Lights and consolations*, which clarify our understanding and move our will

The first criterion, that of revealed commands, calls for our obedience. The second, more rational one requires the exercise of the virtue of prudence. And the third one involves discerning spirits.

If it were only God who moved the soul, there would be nothing to discern. Discernment exists because the evil spirit and our own fallen nature can entice us and push us toward evil, toward a lesser good or toward an apparent greater good. Then how can we discern the movements that agitate our hearts? By using the criteria for spiritual discernment of spirits.

The Absolute Criterion

Jesus Christ, the only one who has seen the Father and is one with him in the Spirit, is by that very fact the only person who knows the Father's will. Therefore, Christ is the absolute criterion of any discernment. Our attitude to Christ lets us discern the presence or absence of God's Spirit.

> Therefore I tell you that nobody speaking by the spirit of God says, "Jesus be accursed." And no one can say, "Jesus is Lord," except by the Holy Spirit.[58]

> When he comes, the Spirit of truth, he will guide you to all truth. He will not speak on his own, but he will speak what he hears, and will declare to you the things that are coming.

58. 1 Cor 12:3.

He will glorify me, because he will take from what is mine
and declare it to you. Everything that the Father has is mine;
for this reason I told you that he will take from what is mine
and declare it to you.[59]

Basic Criteria

Jesus' mind, feelings, and way of acting are written down
in the New Testament, with the result that we find in him the
fundamental criteria for discerning between salvation and con-
demnation. Our following of Christ, our conformity to him, can
only produce good fruits, that is, the fruits of the Spirit:

> The fruit of the Spirit is love, joy, peace, patience, kindness,
> generosity, faithfulness, gentleness, self-control. . . . If we
> live in the Spirit, let us also follow the Spirit.[60]

The Holy Spirit is the gift of God's love,[61] which is why the Spirit
always gives birth to love. Where there is no love, everything is
useless, even the most spectacular actions. Love always reveals
the Spirit of God:

> If I speak in human and angelic tongues, but do not have
> love, I am a resounding gong or a clashing cymbal. And if I
> have the gift of prophecy, and comprehend all mysteries and
> all knowledge; if I have all faith so as to move mountains,
> but do not have love, I am nothing. If I give away everything
> I own, and if I hand my body over to be burned, but do not
> have love, I gain nothing. Love is patient, love is kind. It is
> not jealous, is not pompous, it is not inflated, it is not rude,
> it does not seek its own interests, it is not quick-tempered,
> it does not brood over injury, it does not rejoice over wrong-
> doing but rejoices with the truth. It bears all things, believes
> all things, hopes all things, endures all things.[62]

59. John 16:13-15.
60. Gal 5:22-23, 25.
61. See Rom 5:5.
62. 1 Cor 13:1-7.

> Beloved, let us love one another, because love is of God;
> everyone who loves is begotten by God and knows God.
> Whoever is without love does not know God, for God is
> love. . . .[63]

The criteria of love are the criteria of the Spirit. The sign by which the disciples of Jesus Christ are recognized as such is the love they have for each other.[64] The same Spirit who breathes into each individual person is the soul of the Mystical Body of Christ, the church. Therefore everything that builds up and contributes to the peace and unity of the church comes from the Holy Spirit.[65]

The entire first letter of St. John is a treatise on spiritual discernment, as a single reading of it shows. The Johannine criterion of discernment is simple: if we are children of God, we should act like God. God is light, justice, and love—love, justice, and light manifested in Jesus Christ. Those who are born of God walk in light, justice, and love, just as Christ did. Those who walk in any other way are not children of God, but of the devil!

Primary Criteria

The fundamental criteria offered by the New Testament are channeled to us and made concrete by the chief criteria expressed in its spiritual tradition. Among these criteria the foremost are those offered by St. Ignatius in his book of *Spiritual Exercises*. We follow his teaching here and present below some criteria or rules that will let us not only feel or become aware of the agitations and movements within us, but also come to know their origin and direct them, so that we can embrace the good movements and reject the bad ones.

Times of Spiritual Combat

A first series of criteria is useful, above all, for beginners who are usually in situations of spiritual struggle. So it is advisable

63. 1 John 4:7-21.
64. See John 13:35.
65. See 1 Cor 14.

to present these criteria pedagogically as soon as these persons begin to be stirred up by different spirits.[66] This is obviously a typical situation of any beginner in the following of the Lord Jesus. Novices and simply professed of our monasteries are witnesses of this combat experience. Saint Ignatius offers us two types of rules for the time of struggle. The first type is instructive, the second is directive.

Informative Rules

The informative rules have the purpose of helping us become aware of and distinguish the different movements stirring in the heart. The first two rules refer to persons and the inner movements they experience. The third and fourth ones instruct us about the nature of spiritual consolation and desolation. Here is what Ignatius writes:

> *Rule 1*: In the case of those who go from one mortal sin to another, the enemy is ordinarily accustomed to propose apparent pleasures. He fills their imagination with sensual delights and gratifications, the more readily to keep them in their vices and increase the number of their sins. With such persons the good spirit uses a method which is the reverse of the above. Making use of the light of reason, he will rouse the sting of conscience and fill them with remorse.[67]
>
> *Rule 2*: In the case of those who go on earnestly striving to cleanse their souls from sin and who seek to rise in the service of God to greater perfection, the method pursued is the opposite of that mentioned in the first rule. Then it is characteristic of the evil spirit to harass with anxiety, to afflict with sadness, to raise obstacles backed by fallacious reasonings that disturb the soul. Thus he seeks to prevent the soul from advancing. It is characteristic of the good spirit, however, to give courage and strength, consolations, tears, inspirations,

66. See St. Ignatius, *Spiritual Exercises*, 313–27.
67. Ibid., 314.

and peace. This He does by making everything easy, by removing all obstacles so that the soul goes forward in doing
good.[68]

Rule 3: I call it consolation when an interior movement is
aroused in the soul, by which it is inflamed with love of its
Creator and Lord, and as a consequence, can love no creature on the face of the earth for its own sake, but only in the
Creator of them all. It is likewise consolation when one
sheds tears that move to the love of God, whether it be
because of sorrow for sins, or because of the sufferings of
Christ our Lord, or for any other reason that is immediately
directed to the praise and service of God. Finally, I call consolation every increase of faith, hope, and love, and all interior joy that invites and attracts to what is heavenly and
to the salvation of one's soul by filling it with peace and
quiet in its Creator and Lord.[69]

Rule 4: I call desolation what is entirely the opposite of what
is described in the third rule. It is darkness of soul, turmoil
of spirit, inclination to what is low and earthly, restlessness
rising from many disturbances and temptations which lead
to want of faith, want of hope, want of love. The soul is
wholly slothful, tepid, sad, and separated, as it were, from
its Creator and Lord. For just as consolation is the opposite
of desolation, so the thoughts that spring from consolation
are the opposite of those that spring from desolation.[70]

Directive Rules

The other ten rules of this first series are totally or to a great
extent directive, that is, they teach how to act spiritually, supporting God's work and rejecting that of the evil spirit. Synthetically, they say the following:

68. Ibid., 315.
69. Ibid., 316.
70. Ibid., 317.

Rules 5–9.[71] In times of desolation I must learn to:

Persevere and stay steady in my previous commitments.

Not pay attention to the thoughts that rise from the desolation.

Desire, ask, and work so as to be consoled rapidly.

Seek to get out from under the desolation by prayer and a review of my life.

Examine the possible causes of the desolation:

> Negligence in my life of asceticism and prayer?
> A trial to test my generosity in the service of the Lord?
> A lesson concerning vainglory?

Be patient in suffering, trusting and hoping in grace, which will never fail me.

Rules 10 and 11.[72] In times of consolation I must learn to:

Regain strength for the next desolation.

Humbly recognize that consolation is a free gift.

Remember how powerless I am in desolation, though in grace I can do everything.

Rules 12, 13, and 14.[73] In times of temptation I must learn to:

Reject it strongly and at once.

Open myself to the spiritual accompanist.

Recognize my weak sides.

Consolation and Desolation

The topic of consolations and desolations deserves further clarification. We will treat it here without pretending to say everything on the subject and with the intention of coming back to the topic later from a very special angle.

Any *consolation* substantially consists in a perceptible interior movement toward the Father, together with the experience that

71. Ibid., 318–22.
72. Ibid., 323–24.
73. Ibid., 325–27.

only in him can we love everything he has created. This experience produces a whole series of inner vibrations.

I think that it is important to distinguish between consolation and euphoria. In the former, the feelings stirred up are altruistic, whereas in euphoria they are self-centered. The peace proper to consolation cannot be reduced to a mere feeling of well-being.

Consolations are always an invitation from the Lord to move higher, beyond where we are. They give us the support we need for the long, painful process of purification, which any life in the Spirit demands. They contribute greatly to the transformation of the heart, since they draw it back to its center and bring out its hidden capacities for what is infinite, eternal, absolute.

It is well known that spiritual consolation occupies an important place in St. Bernard's doctrine on monastic life. The Abbot of Clairvaux was aware of it from his own experience and from that of others: "I know how necessary for you is the consolation coming down from heaven, since it is certain that you have manfully sworn off all carnal pleasures and earthly allurements."[74] His basic principle is this: "Holy delight assuredly turns away from the mind preoccupied with worldly desires. . . . Consequently, you cannot equally savor the things above and the things on earth."[75] As for the content of consolation, Bernard expresses it like this:

> "Blessed are they that mourn, for they shall be comforted." What else is this promised comfort but the grace of devotion springing from the hope of pardon, the sweet delight found in well-doing, and the relish of true wisdom—even though very limited—with which the kind Lord sometimes refreshes the soul during her earthly pilgrimage? Yet such a foretaste has no other purpose than to increase our desire of heaven and intensify our love.[76]

74. St. Bernard, *Sermon on Malachy*, 1, 1.
75. St. Bernard, *Ascension*, 6:8. See also 3:6-7.
76. St. Bernard, *All Saints*, 1:10.

We should note that for St. Bernard consolation is nothing else than devotion, which means the gift of self to the Lord. In the same way, St. Ignatius has the essence of consolation consist in the growth of the theological virtues. Both of them totally thwart the temptation to "love the consolations of God, and not the God of consolations."[77]

Desolation—from the Latin word *desolare*, to abandon, to leave alone—basically consists in the loss of any feeling of God's presence and love, together with the complex repercussions that this loss occasions on all levels of one's being. In spiritual desolation, the loss or absence concerns another Person. This is how it differs from mere depression, where the depressed feelings are centered on self.

Desolations are also special occasions for growing in self-knowledge. They favor the experience of "being little or nothing," and thus destroy falsehood and delusions of grandeur. In the same way, they indirectly promote growth by making us long for truth and for what does not pass away.

Nights and Depression

In the context of desolation it is worth saying something concerning the dryness and aridity caused by the *night* of initial infused contemplation. The doctrine of St. John of the Cross is the classical reference on this point. It is important not to confuse this night with desolation. The cause of the night is growth in a purer faith and more self-sacrificing love. The criteria for discerning this painful gift are the following:

— No pleasure or consolation is found, either in the things of God, or in those of the world.

— The remembrance of the Lord is painful and you feel that you are not advancing in it, but rather getting worse, even though you really want to advance.

---

77. See St. Francis de Sales, *Introduction to the Devout Life*, 4, 13: "not the comfort, but the Comforter."

— It is impossible to use your faculties freely during the time dedicated to prayer.

— There is a type of deep, hidden peace in God, together with the desire to rest in him.

The combined presence of these four criteria favors a correct discernment, but what does prudent behavior consist of in this situation? Provided that one is open with another person who has experience, it is advisable to:

— Persevere humbly and patiently in your life of prayer.

— Abandon yourself peacefully and lovingly into the hands of God the Father.

— Cooperate by repeating simple acts of faith, hope, and love insofar as you can, and in the way you can.

Similarly, it is also important to distinguish between the experience of the passive night of the senses—or that of feeling depressed—and the reality of a clinical depression. Below are the chief characteristics of these situations.

The Desert and/or Feeling Depressed	A Clinical Depression
Perceiving that you are on a journey toward a goal	Perceiving that you are going in circles, without any sense of direction
Seeing the fruits of your conversion	Absence of all fruit of any type whatsoever
Normal fulfillment of your activities in other areas outside of prayer	Attention centered on self, which blocks all other activity

It is probable that an experience of feeling depressed and/or some degree of clinical depression also becomes present during a real spiritual night. In such a case it is important to advise the person to do what is best on a practical, concrete level.

Advice for someone clinically *depressed*:

— The person needs to accept his or her suffering, with the insinuation that the cause does not seem to be something spiritual.

— Draw out and spell out all the positive aspects of the depressed person's spiritual life and prayer.

— Help to nourish the person's prayer and life in the Spirit.

— Avoid giving (psychological) advice that the person cannot carry out.

— Send the person to a specialist to receive the necessary help.

Advice for someone in the *night* and also *depressed*:

— Discern and help the person to accept the suffering that comes merely from a psychological factor.

— Help the person face the spiritual desert, emphasizing everything that is positive and authentic in his or her spiritual life and inviting the person to persevere in the life of the search for God, supporting his or her struggle against temptation.

— Accompany the person with the help of a psychologist in whom you trust.

Unfortunately, many persons abandon the road of prayer and even all life in the Spirit, precisely when they are advancing and growing. How much better it would be for them to pray with William of Saint-Thierry:

> Forgive me, Lord, forgive my heart's impatience for you; I seek your face. By your own gift I seek your countenance, lest you should turn it from me at the last. I know indeed and I am sure that those who walk in the light of your countenance do not fall but walk in safety, and by your face their every judgment is directed. They are the living people, for

their life is lived according to what they read and see in your face, as in a paradigm. Lord, I dare not look upon your face against your will, lest I be further confounded. Needy and beggared and blind, I stand in your presence, seen by you though I do not see you. Standing like this, I offer you my heart full of desire for you, the whole of whatever I am, the whole of whatever I can do, the whole of whatever I know, and the very fact that I so yearn and faint for you. But the way to find you, that I do not find![78]

When Peace Is Threatened

The second series of rules from St. Ignatius is "for a more accurate discernment of spirits."[79] It is meant more specifically for those already growing in the spiritual life and for those considerably advanced in it. These rules should be offered when such people begin to suffer temptations "under the appearance of good,"[80] that is, when Satan comes in "the appearance of an angel of light."[81] Putting this into a monastic context, the situation is typical of what often happens after perpetual profession and during subsequent years.

Applying these rules is more difficult than using the ones contained in the first series. They presuppose a certain experience of discretion, that is, of the discretion learned during the time of spiritual struggle. Three of these rules teach us something about the action of the different spirits:

> *Rule 1*: It is characteristic of God and His Angels, when they act upon the soul, to give true happiness and spiritual joy, and to banish all the sadness and disturbances which are caused by the enemy. It is characteristic of the evil one to fight against such happiness and consolation by proposing fallacious reasonings, subtleties, and continual deceptions.[82]

78. William of Saint-Thierry, *Meditations*, 3:3.
79. St. Ignatius, *Spiritual Exercises*, 328.
80. Ibid., 10.
81. Ibid., 328–36.
82. Ibid., 329.

Rule 4: It is a mark of the evil spirit to assume the appearance of an angel of light. He begins by suggesting thoughts that are suited to a devout soul, and ends by suggesting his own. For example, he will suggest holy and pious thoughts that are wholly in conformity with the sanctity of the soul. Afterwards, he will endeavor little by little to end by drawing the soul into his hidden snares and evil designs.[83]

Rule 7: In souls that are progressing to greater perfection, the action of the good angel is delicate, gentle, delightful. It may be compared to a drop of water penetrating a sponge. The action of the evil spirit upon such souls is violent, noisy, and disturbing. It may be compared to a drop of water falling upon a stone. In souls that are going from bad to worse, the action of the spirits mentioned above is just the reverse. The reason for this is to be sought in the opposition or similarity of these souls to the different kinds of spirits. When the disposition is contrary to that of the spirits, they enter with noise and commotion that are easily perceived. When the disposition is similar to that of the spirits, they enter silently, as one coming into his own house when the doors are open.[84]

These three instructions are completed by two directive rules, which teach us how to act with discretion. Here they are in synthetic form:

Rules 5 and 6: In consolation and desolation, one must learn to observe the beginning, middle and end of one's thoughts:[85]

If the growth of the thoughts is entirely healthy, it is a sign of a good spirit and I can trust them.

If the thoughts lead to something evil, less good, or distracting, or if they take my peace away, it is a sign of an evil spirit and I should reject them.

83. Ibid., 332.
84. Ibid., 335.
85. Ibid., 333–34.

Once the situation is passed and in order to gain experience, it helps to look at what happened so as to understand how the evil spirit played his tricks.

Finally, Ignatius enters into a more delicate subject. He refers to what can come before a consolation and offers three important rules, of which two are instructive and the third directive. He says that only God can console someone without a preceding cause, whereas both a good spirit and an evil one can console someone through a preceding cause, although they have contrary goals in mind. When the consolation lacks a cause, one should look at what happens during it and afterwards, since what happens afterwards can come from different spirits. Here is what Ignatius himself says:

> *Rule 2*: God alone can give consolation to the soul without any previous cause. It belongs solely to the Creator to come into a soul, to leave it, to act upon it, to draw it wholly to the love of His Divine Majesty. I said without previous cause, that is, without any preceding perception or knowledge of any subject by which a soul might be led to such a consolation through its own acts of intellect and will.[86]

> *Rule 3*: If a cause precedes, both the good angel and the evil spirit can give consolation to a soul, but for a quite different purpose. The good angel consoles for the progress of the soul, that it may advance and rise to what is more perfect. The evil spirit consoles for purposes that are the contrary, and that afterwards he might draw the soul to his own perverse intentions and wickedness.[87]

> *Rule 8*: When consolation is without previous cause, as was said, there can be no deception in it, since it can proceed from God our Lord only. But a spiritual person who has received such a consolation must consider it very attentively, and must cautiously distinguish the actual time of the consolation from the period which follows it. At such a

86. Ibid., 330.
87. Ibid., 331.

time the soul is still fervent and favored with the grace and aftereffects of the consolation which has passed. In this second period the soul frequently forms various resolutions and plans which are not granted directly by God our Lord. They may come from our own reasoning on the relations of our concepts and on the consequences of our judgments, or they may come from the good or evil spirit. Hence, they must be carefully examined before they are given full approval and put into execution.[88]

Let us pause for a moment here and clarify more precisely the experience that St. Ignatius calls "consolation without previous cause." The theological foundation of this experience of "direct" communication between God and his creature is undeniable. The triune God is a related God—in the divine Persons among themselves—and a relational God toward the human being created in his image and likeness. The Second triune Person, the Son, has become human so as to dwell among us and show us what divine love is. The Third triune Person, the Holy Spirit, has been sent to indwell our hearts together with the Father and the Son. God, who is present within us, can show himself directly in our consciousness and in our moral conscience. However, the problem we are now discussing is more practical than theoretical. The important factor is to understand the phrase "without previous cause." Ignatius explains it twice, so as not to leave any doubts about it. These are the essential points:

— "Without any *preceding*": discretion is needed to be able to affirm that no cause has preceded the consolation

— "Perception or knowledge of any *subject*": that is, an object capable of consoling, such as holy images or an interesting life of a holy person

— "By which a soul *might be led* to such a consolation": once again, discretion is needed to make sure that there has not actually been a mediating subject or object

88. Ibid., 336.

— "Through its own *acts* of intellect and will": some antecedent spiritual exercise, such as *lectio divina*, can also be a cause of consolation, by providing a subject

To sum up, we can say that "preceding" or "previous" means two things: something antecedent in time and something that is also the cause or intermediary of the consolation. Obviously, only the person who experiences the consolation will be able to determine whether or not there has been something previous, as an object or in the subject, and whether it has a causal relation with the consolation in question. The absence of a cause indicates that the consolation is from God.

Take note, however, that Ignatius reminds us how important it is to distinguish the time of the consolation itself and the subsequent time in which the soul continues to feel the consequences of fervor and light coming from that consolation. What makes itself present to one's awareness in the following moment may come from either a good spirit or a bad one, not necessarily nor immediately from God. As we have said, the devil often disguises himself as an angel of light.

Vocational Criteria

Vocational discernment is a vast and complex topic. We here reduce it to a single aspect, that of the vocational criteria used in this type of discernment.

Both abundance and lack of vocations often provoke a greater emphasis on the importance of discernment. The lack of vocations pushes us toward running imprudent risks so as to give doubtful candidates a trial, whereas abundance leads us to neglect removing the weeds from the harvest.

Benedictine Criteria:

Patient Perseverance

We begin by presenting four general criteria that St. Benedict gives in his Rule. The first one is at the beginning of chapter 58:

> When someone comes first to the monastic life, he should
> not be allowed entry too readily, but as the Apostle says,
> "Test whether the spirits be godly."[89] Thus if the newcomer
> perseveres in knocking and is seen to bear patiently for four
> or five days the rebuffs offered him and the difficulty of
> entrance, and if he persists in his request, then let him come
> in and stay in the guest room for a few days.[90]

We have here an initial discernment, the object of which is to see
if the candidate is moved by the Spirit of God. It is in this context
and to help in this discernment that Benedict offers two criteria
that are easy to observe, namely, whether he "perseveres in
knocking" and whether he does this "patiently." The time factor
will also help to verify both realities. If the candidate shows perseverance in his request and patience in waiting for a few days,
then it could be affirmed that God's Spirit has brought him to
the monastery. Of course, this does not mean that he should immediately embrace monastic life.

Note in passing the stress on patience from the very start of
monastic life. Without patience, there is no participation in the
redeeming passion of Christ, nor any deeply merciful communion
in the weaknesses of the members of the community.[91] We could
even go so far as to say that patience—with oneself and with
others—is a prime factor for persevering in the monastic life.

True Search for God

The second Benedictine criterion is this: "One must note
whether he really seeks God, and whether he is serious about the
Work of God, obedience and hardships."[92] In this context, the search
for God does not mean looking for a hidden God, but for a God

89. 1 John 4:1.
90. RB 58.1-4.
91. See ibid., Prol. 50 and 72.5.
92. Ibid., 58.7.

from whom we had strayed and to whom we have decided to return, a God who anticipated our search and first sought us.[93]

Benedict says that "one must note (*sollicitudo sit*)." The impersonal form gives the impression that the agent who notes the fulfillment of the three parts of this discernment criterion is each member of the community. The obligation implied here can be understood as that of attentive watching. Such solicitude refers to the intensity of the observation to be made, but above all to its duration. What subtle solicitude does not achieve will be easily obtained by the passage of time. Time reveals the secret of hearts.

The object of the attentive watching is not the invisible intention of the candidate to enter monastic life, but his or her visible behavior. This is judged from a triple perspective, namely, giving oneself to a life of prayer, embracing someone else's will rather than one's own, and accepting everything that puts pride down. We can note in passing that it is not a question of simply giving oneself to prayer, obedience, and humility but of a "solicitous," fervent, dedicated gift and acceptance, full of good zeal. An act of personal commitment with these characteristics almost speaks for itself.

It is not by chance that *prayer* occupies the first place. Benedict is consistent with what he said at the very start of the Rule: "First, when you set out to do some good work, beg him with most insistent prayer to bring it to completion."[94] So that it will be beyond discussion, he will state with total clarity, "Nothing should be put ahead of the Work of God."[95] Nevertheless, we should remember that *Opus Dei* refers to the Divine Office in its relation to all the personal effort of general attention to God.[96]

Benedictine *obedience* is a result of prayer,[97] which is why it has a certain primacy: "The first degree of humility is obedience without delay."[98] Such obedience conforms and unites the can-

93. Ibid., Prol. 2, 14; 58.8.
94. Ibid., Prol. 4.
95. Ibid., 43.3.
96. See ibid., 19.1-2; 7.10, ff.
97. See ibid., 6.2.
98. Ibid., 5.1.

didate to Jesus Christ, who said, "I have not come to do my will, but that of him who sent me."[99]

If we take into account the possible source of this text in St. Basil the Great,[100] *humiliations* refer to the modest, mundane chores considered as degrading by the secular society of that time. It is not a question of being purposefully and intentionally humiliated, but of accepting a life of simple service. Monastic life itself will see to it that our humility is helped by humiliation.[101] This is how the candidate to monastic life begins to cling to Christ, who shows himself as "meek and humble of heart," as having come to serve and not to be served.[102]

Saint Benedict is very concrete. The search for God is made evident by searching for him, which includes struggling with our self-centeredness and pride, because it is these that block our communion with Christ and with our neighbor. Perhaps the words of our monastic Father could be reformulated in the following two questions: Does the candidate to monastic life want to follow Christ and imitate him in prayer, obedience, and self-emptying? Are the candidate's prayer, obedience, and humility really at the service of his or her search for God?

It is also worth noting that these three Benedictine signs of the true search for God correspond somewhat to the steps of humility. Thus the first step of humility describes the monk's relation to God; the second, third, and fourth steps are degrees of obedience; and steps five through eight propose forms of self-abasement related to opprobrium and humiliations. For reasons that we do not know—perhaps they were literary or pedagogical—Benedict says nothing about taciturnity or silence as a vocational criterion. Steps nine through twelve of the ladder of humility, however, speak of this quality of the monk.[103]

99. Ibid., 7.32. John 6:38.
100. See Basil, *Rule (Small Asceticon)*, 7.
101. See RB 7.44-54.
102. See Matt 11:29; Mark 10:45.
103. See RB 7.56-66.

Observing the Rule

The third key criterion for vocational discernment comes from confronting the candidate with the community's rule of monastic life. Saint Benedict says that his Rule should be read three times in its entirety to the candidate before making a final promise. His patient observance of it constitutes another criterion for vocational discernment.[104]

Benedict is very practical when it comes to discerning vocations. The candidate's intentions have to be embodied in humble, obedient behavior, and this behavior needs to be verified by the observance of the entire Rule, thus becoming a further proof of the candidate's search for God.

Good Zeal

The solicitude for monastic life, which the candidate is to show, is intimately linked to the good zeal belonging to someone who decides to withdraw from vice and run on the path toward God. That is why we can think that chapter 72 of the Rule, on good zeal and ardent love, embodies the final criteria for verifying the true gift of self and one's growth in divine life. These criteria, inherent in good zeal, can be presented synthetically as follows:

— Mutual respect (honor)

— Mutual support (patience)

— Mutual obedience (obedience)

— Self-denial, not denial of one's neighbor! (mortification-sacrifice)

— Mutual love (brotherhood, sisterhood)

— Loving fear of God (beginning of wisdom)

— Unfeigned love of the abbot/abbess (filial piety)

— Preferring nothing whatever to his only Son! (Christo-centrism)

104. See ibid., 58.9-16.

A novice, either monk or nun, who is not aflame at least sometimes with ardent zeal, thus running the risk of sinning by indis-
cretion, runs the other risk of becoming a mediocre solemnly
professed. Popular wisdom translates this as, "A new broom
sweeps clean and an old donkey sits still."

It is obvious that these four criteria, especially that of good
zeal, are valid not only for entrance into monastic life, but also
for perseverance in it and for the final entry of monks and nuns
into eternal life.

Admission

The teachings given above by St. Benedict should be kept in
mind and retranslated into the circumstances of today's world.
They keep all their value, thanks, above all, to their foundation
in the gospel, although the precise form in which the principles
are incarnated can change and be enriched.

Discernment for admission to monastic life is not easy and in
some way this difficulty helps justify our many mistakes. There are
usually many motivations working at the time of entry into a monastery, motivations that are both natural and spiritual. It is difficult
to discern the action of God in the complex combination of attractions that the candidate experiences. And it is easy to think that
every attraction to a deeper, more permanent life of prayer connotes
a vocation to monastic life. However, the failure of many consecrated persons in other forms of life who have attempted to transfer
to us is sufficient to make us question such a way of thinking.

The church's centuries-old wisdom contained in the new
Code of Canon Law reminds us that a special vocation is needed
to enter any form of consecrated life: "Certain Christian faithful
are specially called to this state by God so that they may enjoy a
special gift in the life of the Church."[105] To say "special" is the
equivalent of saying *rare, not frequent.* Actually, less than one in
a thousand baptized Christians are chosen for such a vocation,

---

105. Code, c. 574.2.

and even less as regards the monastic vocation. Perhaps we do not like it, but we have to say that in the church a monk or nun is a *rara avis*, an exotic bird.

Therefore, the possibility of a divine call must be examined seriously. In many cases, professional help will be needed to discern unconscious, more or less self-centered motivations, which prevent a truly free decision by the candidate. This reality makes us face a delicate question, namely the advisability, or not, of a psychological test at the very start of the vocational process.

It is obvious that the psychologist does not have the last word, but it seems important to point out the help that psychology can bring to vocational discernment. A psychological diagnosis can help in evaluating the presence or absence of the necessary prerequisites for embracing our particular type of life. This evaluation then aids us in arriving at a better judgment concerning the candidate's health or pathology, and in clarifying both the areas that need attention and the best methods for the future formation process. In other words, we are trying to clarify our replies to the following questions:

— Is the person basically free to make this decision, or are there some pathological dynamics —either actively at work or latent—that argue against the inner freedom of such a decision?

— To what extent is the person really free to give him or herself and to cooperate fully and wholeheartedly with God's interior work?

— What tensions or difficulties can be foreseen in the future?

— What areas of the candidate's personality seem to need the work of an evangelical revision and reintegration?

Experience in the field of discernment of monastic vocations has helped me establish some signs, or criteria, which can point to a divine calling:

— Sincere desire to embrace the life of the community as a means for going to God

— Humble docility based on faith, in learning to live as a monk or nun

— Capacity for solitude without self-marginalization, and for solidarity without dependencies

— Physical, mental, and affective health, so as to live this life fruitfully

We give first place to the "cenobitic criteria," since it is through them that the authenticity of the newcomer's search for God is most easily verified. Let us not forget that Benedict wrote his Rule for the "most vigorous race, the cenobites."[106]

A sincere love of one's particular community despite its poverty and weakness is a good sign with which to begin. So is the *desire to learn*, expressed by letting oneself be taught. Those who, before entering, have devoured monastic literature and therefore know it all are very likely to . . . And finally, relationships say a lot about someone's heart.

Concerning psychological health, our opinion is that, for the reasons already expressed above, a competent diagnosis can often be advisable. The affective maturity that is necessary at the start basically consists in a certain stability of emotional states, peaceful identification with one's own sex, capacity to welcome others as different, and the openness to fruitfulness beyond what is physical and bodily.

We have just said, "peaceful identification with one's own sex." What does that mean? We leave to one side the presence of a certain eroticism toward persons of one's own sex. This phenomenon is fairly common in passing from a familiar set of relationships into a community. The sudden absence of normal affection looks for some form of expression among the persons of the community. Such a passing phenomenon can recur every

106. RB 1.13.

now and then, but it has nothing to do with homosexuality, of which we will speak below. This disorientation and reorientation of affection can often be more common among women, which does not mean that it is totally absent among men.

Our problem is different and can be expressed in the question, How can the vocation of persons with a homosexual or lesbian tendency be discerned? If we speak of discernment, we are already presuming that there are persons in this situation who can be truly called to monastic life by the Lord, and that they not only can be called, but also have given a positive response to this call and follow the Lord in our form of life.

We know that this subject usually stirs up people's emotions and provokes a certain nervousness. It is probable that from this point on, readers will be on edge to see what position I am going to take. In fact, it is even probable that some readers' emotions replace these reflections! So let me begin with a statement that I hope will be generally accepted, namely, that many men and women suffer deeply and feel rejected because of their homosexuality. If we want to live as Christians, we must welcome them most respectfully and unite ourselves with their pain. These persons who have a homosexual orientation live their condition in different ways. Some do so with a strong sense of guilt, rejection, and secrecy. Others have achieved a serene sense of acceptance, trust, and integration into ordinary life. This integration of sexuality is extremely important, both for homosexuals and for heterosexuals.

Here is a basic criterion: those persons who have not arrived at dominating their homosexual tendencies are automatically excluded. Actually, the same principle should be applied to those who have not yet dominated their heterosexual attraction.[107] "Dominate" here means not only the effort of the will, but also a gradual freedom from the tendency itself, in such a way that the latter gradually lessens its influence on one's life and lets the person develop the duties of state with neither excessive tension

107. See CIVCSVA, *Guidelines for Formation in Religious Institutes*, 39.

nor undue monopolization of his or her attention in a compulsive or permanent way.

If there is real self-dominion in this area on the part of a homosexual candidate, plus a genuine attraction to monastic life, the following areas will have to be studied:

— The degree of mature appropriation of the person's own sexuality, knowing especially that this will be more difficult in a predominately masculine or feminine life situation.

— The degree to which the candidate has shed light on his or her image of father and mother. Since this image can often be negative and dominating, it needs to be elaborated so as to permit a normal relationship with authority and an interiorly peaceful obedience.

— The capacity to clarify and put in order one's feelings of jealousy and one's need for affectionate support, so as to be able to live in peace and let others do the same.

— The motivation for wanting to embrace celibacy, and the sincere esteem for it as a life option, in view of the fact that the candidate's situation in an exclusively male or female milieu will demand a significantly greater effort.

— The capacity to relate with young people of either sex.

It could be thought that this more careful discernment is due to a *homophobic* mentality, an aversion to gay or homosexual people. Exactly the opposite is true. Someone with a homosexual tendency is, before all and above all, a human person. The respect that the person deserves implies guaranteeing the necessary help and thus presenting truthfully and lovingly the difficulties that he or she is going to find in a life of interpersonal relations in community. Besides, monastic tradition emphasizes that any newcomer "should not be allowed entry too readily" and should be clearly told beforehand about "all the hard and harsh things that lead to God."[108]

108. RB 58.1, 8.

Of course, any type of gay pride within the monastic life can only be damaging to everyone, at least because it puts the emphasis on sexual orientation rather that on the more global identity of the person. At the other extreme, however, to treat the topic of sexuality as taboo is often very harmful for persons with such an orientation, since a climate of denial or secrecy makes the process of recognizing and integrating the tendency much more difficult. Such a climate becomes the cause of repression, guilt complexes, and other pathologies. The homosexual condition, when circumstances help the process, can be accepted and integrated. This requires effort, just as integration of affectivity and sexuality require effort on the part of a heterosexual person.

In this context, a word should be said about lesbianism, that is, feminine homosexuality or the orientation of the woman's sexuality toward a person of her own sex. Actually, it does not seem to be correct to speak of homosexuality as a generic phenomenon with two species: male and female. Lesbianism is very often *homophilia*, love of a woman for a woman, without necessarily implying a genital factor. Precisely for that reason, because it is more often concentrated on affection than on the body, lesbianism tends to be more socially accepted than is male homosexuality. Consequently, vocational discernment will look more closely at the quality of the candidate's relationships than at control of the sexual drive. Mention should also be made of homophobia among heterosexuals who do not adequately integrate their openness to a man, and also among homosexuals who reject their own condition. This, however, would take us away from the simpler subject we are studying here.

Finally, we should say that the decision of the abbot or abbess in the admission of a candidate is the decisive factor in the discernment process, because no one has a right to be admitted and only a fool could think that one can impose his or her own vocation on the community! An over-conviction about one's own calling and its imposition on others is a sign of not having been called.

Novitiate

These criteria for admission are equally valid for beginning the novitiate. During this stage of formation, the criterion consists solely in the reality of growth. This growth should be verified in its two dimensions: human and spiritual. Human growth must be integral, that is, in its multiple aspects: intellectual, volitional, affective, interpersonal, social, working, and transcendent. We will speak of this very shortly.

Spiritual growth, on the other hand, is shown in one's interpersonal relationship with Jesus Christ, which is of capital importance. We have to keep in mind that the final object of monastic life is none other than conformity to the Lord and communion with everyone in him. Only he brings us all together to eternal life. If this double growth is really taking place, the novice can be considered ready for the gift of self, to Christ and to the community, through temporary monastic profession.

Profession

We look now at the situation of the temporarily professed in the monasticate as they prepare for perpetual monastic profession. Their progress during the three years of temporary profession needs to be determined in relation to prayer, work, acceptance of corrections, relations with the superiors and with the members of the community, emotional and temperamental control, and human maturity. All these elements, when positive, are signs of cooperation with the vocational grace they have received.

At the end of the period of temporary profession, the young professed will freely ask the abbot or abbess for solemn profession. The latter, together with the junior director, will discern the request. At that important moment in monastic formation, what are the criteria to be used?

As we understand it, the criteria concern three realities: openness to the community, human maturity, and experience in prayer. As regards openness to the community, there is not much to say, because the young professed is either open or not. Any member of the community with a minimum of common sense would be able to answer the following question: Am I integrated into the community?

Human maturity, as we have already seen, is a reality related to the whole of human existence. That is why someone who is intellectually mature but affectively immature is an immature person. Nevertheless, someone affectively mature, even though less mature intellectually, is more mature than the immature person described in the previous sentence. In other words, affective maturity is supremely important. Experience shows that a healthy degree of affective maturity is absolutely necessary for inner freedom and for life in community. Affectivity is the human capacity for experiencing agreeable and disagreeable feelings and for manifesting them by means of emotional reactions that influence the body and the psyche. Persons who enjoy a certain affective maturity usually act, rather than react, which is why they:

— Easily tolerate frustrations: "If I can't have it today, I'll have it tomorrow."

— Control inner impulses and outer pressures: "In spite of everything, I'm free."

— Adapt themselves to changes: "A centered heart soon finds its rest."

— Affirm themselves by lessening their own importance: "I'm not the only one with rights."

— Behave with flexibility: "What is rigid usually breaks in two."

— Are capable of giving and receiving: "I love to welcome others and give myself."

— Accept their sin without any guilt complex: "Through my most grievous fault . . . period!"

— Practice renunciation for a greater cause: "I quit this because I prefer that."

— Take many things in good grace: "My sense of humor acts against my reactions."

Human affectivity and sexuality are supremely relational realities. In monastic life we live them in a celibate way. Many young people, both men and women, have come to the monastery with deep wounds in this basic dimension of human existence. We very often have to help them.

Victims of sexual abuse—usually in the family environment and above all among young girls —are much more common than what appears at first. Statistics say that 80 percent of such victims are girls and 20 percent are boys. In 95 percent of the cases, the abuser is a man and 85 percent of these abusers are identified as a member of the family (uncle, grandfather, brother, father) or a friend of the family. The wounds from abuse last for years and even for the rest of the victim's life, unless he or she breaks the silence and receives adequate assistance. This help will have to aim at the tendency to cover up and protect the abuser; at the feeling of having become a damaged, second-class human being forever; at the difficulty to trust anyone; at the guilty feelings, fears, repressed anger and feeling of hostility; at the fear of intimacy and inability to enjoy anything. This necessary therapeutic help will probably go beyond the possibilities of spiritual accompaniment.

Human sexuality, precisely because it is human, needs to be personalized, which means that it has to be interpreted in the context of one's own personal history. In normal circumstances, the spiritual accompanist should be ready to help by rendering a threefold service:

— Give meaning to what was previously experienced, which is done in the context of a welcoming, enlightening dialogue that lets the accompanied person reveal his or her personal history.

— The narration should favor the discovery of links uniting past experiences to what is being lived today.

— Then the past should be integrated into the project of cenobitic celibacy.

It is much more delicate to establish criteria for verifying theological growth or, more concretely, the deepening of one's prayer life. We can start with some criteria of Christian maturity. The most evident characteristics of mature faith are the following: a clear perception of good and evil, a life centered on the great truths of faith, dependence on divine initiative, total openness to the gospel, affectivity in a state of self-gift, reference to the church, and the discovery of the Eucharist as the source of life.

Let us now look at signs of maturity in the monastic context. In all our communities there is doubtless some member about whom we can say that from his "perfect love of God which drives out fear . . . he can now begin to accomplish effortlessly, as if spontaneously, everything that he previously did out of fear. He will do this no longer out of fear of hell but out of love for Christ, good habit itself and a delight in virtue. Once his worker has been cleansed of vices and sins, the Lord will graciously make all this shine forth in him by the power of the Holy Spirit."[109] But what is it that comes to the surface in such a "worker . . . cleansed of vices and sins"? Their unifying friendship with the Lord shows that their spiritual and monastic life is:

— More like a fountain than a river: it flows from their heart and not through external tributaries

— More open than closed: available to the Spirit's action

— More self-critical than self-justifying: open to discernment

— More unifying than multiplying: reducing many to a few, and a few to one

— More a doer of God's will than a seeker of intimate relationships: committed and self-forgetful

— More humble than dogmatic: with many questions and few answers

109. RB 7.67-70.

— More creative than imitating: acknowledging the freshness of him who makes all things new

Religious maturity and psychological maturity go almost hand in hand. They both spring from the person who is called to integrate all aspects that make up his or her identity. The person who is more balanced and healthy, humanly speaking, has more possibilities of living a fuller and deeper monastic experience. Of course there are exceptions, as there are in all things human, but the exceptions confirm the rule. Yet there is nothing impossible for God.

Clarifications

As a conclusion, we would like to give some clarifications and advice concerning three particular topics: doubtful spirits, little deceptions, and the vicissitudes of life.

Doubtful Spirits

In spiritual discernment, not everything is black and white. There are movements and spirits that are difficult to discern. Tradition has called these spirits "doubtful spirits." Let us look briefly at some examples, which could certainly be multiplied:

— Wanting to change one's state of life after making a previous option, even if the latter had been well discerned. It is not unusual for a cenobite to want to become a hermit.

— A tendency toward what is singular and beyond one's own private competence. What should we think of a nun who wants to make a foundation even against the opinion of all her community?

— Desiring extraordinary feats in the practice of the virtues, such as exaggerated fasts and vigils, that go beyond what is common and ordinary

— Constant sensible consolations or permanent desolation without any type of peace in the Lord

— Extraordinary graces and charisms that are not the fruit of a virtuous interior life, nor show any authentic gift of self to others

— Fraternal correction that is correct, but lacks humble meekness

Discernment often faces its limitations when it comes up against situations like these. In such cases all one can do is wait to judge the spirits by their fruits. No devil can hide his tail forever and only fools, or the proud, mistake his forked tail for a friendly hand.

LITTLE DECEPTIONS

Spiritual error or deception is more frequent than we think. Leaving aside the greater deceits and deceivers—false visionaries, false messengers, etc.—we want to point out some *little deceits* that, however, are dangerous when they become characteristic of a person's spiritual behavior.

It is evident that a deception is an error, which is unnoticed but fed by disordered affections and self-love. A simple mistake, when it is perceived by the intellect, can easily be corrected, but a deception has strong roots that are deeply embedded in a conscious or unconscious attachment to something or to someone. Among the different forms of deception are the following:

— Rejecting as impossible any mystical communication between God and his human creation, together with an absolute denial of the existence and action of demonic spirits

— Self-sufficiently affirming moral and/or doctrinal criteria opposed to authentic tradition and the church's teaching, as expressed by the councils and the popes

— Pretending to refound monastic life, totally abstracting from centuries of experience in the search and discovery of the Lord

— Proclaiming one's monastic vocation even after repeated experiments that ended in failure and were against the prudent opinion of the monastery's superior

— Insisting in a project for a foundation without the backing of the community, contrary to the opinion of competent persons and without the necessary natural and spiritual qualities

— Believing that total fidelity and commitment should be the first step, the fundamental disposition to begin following the Lord, rather than the sincere determination to grow in fidelity and commitment

— Affirming God's presence in one's spiritual experience only because of its intensity and permanence

— Concentrating on secondary attitudes or aspects of Christian and monastic life—liturgical observances, canonical precepts, monastic habit, enclosure—while neglecting the central virtues and attitudes, such as self-denial, humility, spirit of prayer, fraternal service, and a preference for the poor

— Considering that one's monastery is better or more pleasing to God than the others, because of its many vocations and good regular discipline

— Insisting on prudent discretion that maintains one's mediocrity and easy life

— Thinking oneself good or holy because of being accepted, praised, and respected by others

— Emphasizing mystical experience and forgetting committed service to the brothers or sisters

As we have already said, in these cases there is nothing to discern. The mere presence of some of these deceptions under the form of convictions implies a heavy dose of self-love and little love of God and of others.

The conclusion is that the "deceived" person should be helped by healthy doctrine and self-knowledge. Humble openness of heart is the most adequate instrument for killing off deceptions and restoring life to the deceived.

VICISSITUDES OR ALTERNATIONS

We become aware of our journey toward the Lord, thanks to consolations and desolations, presences and absences, hope and fear. Such experiences are necessary for spiritual growth. Saint Bernard of Clairvaux calls these frequent changes of inner spiritual experiences "vicissitudes" or "alternations." Bernard's teaching can shed new light on the topic of spiritual discernment of spirits:

> The person who fears God is initiated into wisdom. He soon reaches maturity and cries out in his fear, "I am at the gates of hell!" The fear of hell takes him away from evil and he begins to look for consolation in what is good, because we all need consolation in one way or another. That consolation which comes from the hope of eternal salvation is very good. It removes the sins that separate the person from God, and divine grace gives him a new life and a new joy. As he progresses, that is to say, to the degree that he lives fervently in Christ, persecution will undoubtedly come his way, as Scripture says. His new joy is then changed into sadness, and the sweetness that had just been in his mouth now becomes bitterness. . . . Tears gush forth because of the lost sweetness, tears that are much more bitter than the ones shed previously for the pain of his sins.
>
> This desolation will be prolonged until God has mercy and consoles the person again. Once peace is recovered, he understands that the temptation he suffered was not abandonment, but a test: a trial that is meant to instruct, not destroy. As Scripture says: "You observe him with each new day and try him at every moment."[110] That is why his new

110. Job 7:18.

awareness of the fruit of temptation makes him want it, not avoid it. And so he says: "Examine me, Lord, and try me."[111] With these continuous vicissitudes from the visits of grace and the trials of temptation, he keeps advancing in the school of virtue. The visit of grace keeps him from fainting, and temptation takes him far away from pride. Such an exercise purifies his inner vision until suddenly light appears. He longs to be swallowed up in it, but the weight of his body drags him down so that, despite his efforts, he falls back again on himself. However, he has already tasted some of the goodness of the Lord, and now returns to his home with this new taste so pleasing to the palate of his heart. From now on he will no longer want any gift, but rather the Giver himself. This is the charity that does not seek its own interests and makes the son abandon his own will for that of his loving Father. Fear, on the contrary, would make the servant look out for his own comfort, and hope would push the hired soldier towards his private booty.[112]

This long quotation lets us draw several important conclusions. The first one is that consolation is very good and desolation very instructive. Without an alternation from one to the other, no growth in the school of virtue is possible, nor will there be any purification of the interior eye and of the desire for God. In fact, without this continual exercise of first one experience, then the other, no one arrives at filial love. This is that love that seeks neither its own interests nor the gifts of God, but longs for God himself. Once again, we see that everything is a gain for the person who truly seeks God:

My perfection will not be based solely on the morning of your visit or on the evening of my trials, but on both of them together. . . . When the morning of grace smiles on me, I will leap for joy and sing a song of thanksgiving for your visit. And when evening comes I will not fail to offer you

111. Ps 26:2.
112. St. Bernard, *Various Sermons*, 3:1.

my evening oblation and, like a mourning dove, shed tears
in my tribulation. Thus my whole life will be for the Lord,
for "at night there are tears, but joy comes with dawn."[113] I
will swallow the bitterness of the night and delight in the
joy of the dawn, because both the contrite sinner and the
justified friend are pleasing to God. In the same way, he
dislikes both the ungrateful friend and the hardened
sinner.[114]

Bernard develops this topic of alternations even more fully
in his sermon 17 on the *Song of Songs*, this time in relation to the
visits and departures of the Holy Spirit. The Spirit "comes and
goes, and if a man can stand firm only with his support, it follows
that he must fall when abandoned by him; fall, yes, but never
fatally, since the Lord supports him by the hand. Persons who
are spiritual or whom the Holy Spirit purposes to make spiritual,
never cease to experience these alternations; he visits them every
morning and tests them at any moment." We must be attentive
to these alternations because, if not, "we shall neither desire him
when he seems absent nor respond to him when present."[115] The
reason for his absence is clear. It is so that we will search for him
with greater longing. The same is true for his presence, which is
to console us. The soul that is not aware of his absence runs the
danger of deceiving itself and of following its own feelings. And
someone who is not aware of the Spirit's return will not be grateful for his visit.

Further on in his commentary, in sermon 74, Bernard returns
to the theme of alternations when speaking about the visits of
the Word. He gives the example of his own experience and con-
fesses that he has frequently been visited by the Word. Nevertheless, in spite of these frequent experiences, he never was aware
of exactly when the Word entered and when he left. Actually, he
neither entered nor left, since "'in him we live and move and

113. Ps 30:6.
114. St. Bernard, *Various Sermons*, 3:3-4.
115. St. Bernard, *On the Song*, 17:1-2.

have our being,'"[116] which is why it is good to know how to recognize his presence. Here are the empirical criteria that the Abbot of Clairvaux offers for recognizing the Word:

> He is life and power, and as soon as he enters in, he awakens my slumbering soul; he stirs and soothes and pierces my heart, for before it was hard as stone, and diseased. So he has begun to pluck out and destroy, to build up and to plant, to water dry places and illuminate dark ones; to open what was closed and to warm what was cold; to make the crooked ways straight and the rough places smooth, so that my soul may bless the Lord, and all that is within me praise his holy name. Thus when the Bridegroom, the Word, came to me, he never made known his coming by any signs, not by sight, not by sound, not by touch. It was not by any movement of his that I recognized his coming; it was not by any of my senses that I perceived he had penetrated to the depths of my being. Only by the movement of my heart, as I have told you, did I perceive his presence; and I knew the power of his might because my faults were put to flight and my human yearnings brought into subjection. I have marveled at the depth of his wisdom when my secret faults have been revealed and made visible; at the very slightest amendment of my way of life I have experienced his goodness and mercy. In the renewal and remaking of the spirit of my mind, that is of my inmost being, I have perceived the excellence of his glorious beauty, and when I contemplate all these things I am filled with awe and wonder at his manifold greatness.[117]

Look now, however, at the opposite experience, that is, what happens in the human heart when the Word is absent or when his presence is not felt:

> But when the Word has left me, all these spiritual powers become weak and faint and begin to grow cold, as though

116. Acts 17:28.
117. St. Bernard, *On the Song*, 74:6.

you had removed the fire from under a boiling pot, and this
is the sign of his going. Then my soul must needs be sor-
rowful until he returns, and my heart again kindles within
me: the sign of his returning.[118]

But why does the Word leave? Bernard answers, "When I have
had such experience of the Word, is it any wonder that I take to
myself the words of the Bride, calling him back when he has
withdrawn? For although my fervor is not as strong as hers, yet
I am transported by a desire like hers. As long as I live the word
'return,' the word of recall for the recall of the Word, will be on
my lips. As often as he slips away from me, so often shall I call
him back. From the burning desire of my heart I will not cease
to call him, begging him to return, as if after someone who is
departing, and I will implore him to give back to me the joy of
his salvation and restore himself to me."[119]

To conclude, the continual experience of alternations between consolations and desolations is itself a criterion of the
authenticity of our life in the Spirit. God is unforeseeable and we
are changeable, deeply in need of purification and support. Absence makes desire grow. It expands the heart. And God is greater
than our hearts.

118. Ibid., 74:7.
119. Ibid.

4

A CONCLUDING LOOK

It is true: God is greater than our hearts. And this book could finish with those words. But we will add some more. It is important to stress and/or to enrich something already said, or at least insinuated.

GRACE AND NATURE

The experience of spiritual accompaniment, paternity or maternity, teaches us that we have to learn to unite what is human with what is divine, grace with nature, but without confusing these two dimensions of reality. In other words, we will clearly distinguish the human and the divine, but without separating them. The best patristic and spiritual theology teaches us these truths, which we must never forget:

Grace presupposes nature. Our natural human qualities are a condition for the work of divine grace. A human being only exists when situated in a concrete existence, which is why grace presupposes the person existing in concrete conditions. These conditions are not only biological, but also psychological, social, cultural, and within the ongoing process of a person's particular history. It is almost impossible to establish the boundary line between the work of grace and the action of nature. God wants, feels, thinks, and loves in us through our desires, affectivity, reason, and will. One monk put it well: "God works and we perspire."

Grace does not destroy nature, but perfects it. There is nothing human that is outside the world of grace, which does not supplant or annul nature, but elevates it. If we believe in God, we have to believe, too, in the human person created in his image and likeness. Divine glory and human happiness are not opposed but, on the contrary, enrich each other. Grace heals our wounds and elevates our capacities. God almost always works his miracles by using us.

Action follows being. The way we act corresponds to the way we are. Grace always acts in a concrete way and this concreteness corresponds to the contextual identity of each human person. There are personal endowments that facilitate the divine work and there exist, on the contrary, personal poverties that weaken the action of grace. The work of grace is normally proportional to the personal unification and freedom of each individual. However, no one is so poor or miserable that God cannot work miracles in that person. Only pride and egoism abort God's plan in our hearts.

These principles from healthy theology and human spiritual experience should encourage us to grow in three ways: to abound in gratitude to God for taking his creation seriously; to abound even more in hope because all things are possible for those who strive to love the Lord; and to imitate divine humility, which hides its work so that others may be praised for it. Without going overboard in search of miracles, we should believe and rejoice in the infinite ordinary miracles that God performs in the routine of our daily lives.

THE RULE, THE ABBOT OR ABBESS, AND ACCOMPANIMENT

The spiritual accompaniment of a cenobitic monk or nun takes place in a very specific context, namely "under a rule and an abbot."[1] One might think that such a normative context would

---

1. T. Kardong, *Benedict's Rule: A Translation and Commentary* (Collegeville, MN: Liturgical Press, 1996), 1.2.

block inner freedom of the Spirit and render all forms of spiritual discernment superfluous, so a clarification needs to be made.

We cenobites have chosen to live under a monastic Rule. This Rule brings an objective dimension to our lives, transmits the essential part of tradition, and provides the rules of the game that have been freely embraced by all the members.[2] "All" here means everyone without exception, namely the abbot,[3] the prior,[4] the deans,[5] the priests,[6] and the novices.[7]

At the same time, however, we know very well that the Rule neither contains nor says everything: "The whole fulfillment of justice is not laid down in this Rule."[8] It is a "modest rule,"[9] drawn up as an introduction for beginners. The weak should find in it a sort of home, in which they "are not overwhelmed," while the strong can be "challenged" to greater things.[10] It is not to be strictly applied to children and the old,[11] which means that there is ample room for the discernment of personal situations and, above all, for spiritual accompaniment after passing through the years of first monastic initiation.

For their part, the abbot and the abbess bring their solicitude for the subjective dimension, their sensitivity to the circumstances, and the possibilities of creative adaptation. They are helped in this by the advice of the brothers and sisters, and by the interior inspiration of grace.[12] In other words, the abbot and abbess are responsible not only for having the Rule lived, but for making it livable in daily life.

2. See ibid., 3.7; 7.55.
3. See ibid., 3.11; 64.20.
4. See ibid., 65.17.
5. See ibid., 62.7.
6. See ibid., 60.2, 9; 62.4, 11.
7. See ibid., 58.10, 15-16.
8. Ibid., 73.Title.
9. Ibid., 73.8.
10. Ibid., 64.19; see also Prol. 47-49; 7.68.
11. See ibid., 37.
12. See ibid., 3.3.

The Rule does not pretend to be more than a practical guide of evangelical life, "with the Gospel as our guide."[13] Sacred Scripture is "a completely reliable guidepost for human life,"[14] which is why St. Benedict sends us to the Gospel and to Jesus Christ. The abbot or abbess takes the place of Christ, is called by his name,[15] and is advised to imitate the example of the Good Shepherd.[16] Both channels of authority are paths to Christ: to his Person, his Word, and his Work. The abbot or abbess and the Rule thus become a single reality. "Under a rule and an abbot" means under the orders and the grace of Christ.

Spiritual accompaniment offers a service of discernment to cenobites, monks, and nuns, so that their regular observance be a true following of the Lord, full of life in the Spirit.

SPIRITUAL MOTHERHOOD

Spiritual paternity and/or maternity always imply some type of accompaniment, but not every form of spiritual accompaniment involves paternity or maternity in the spirit. In other words, fatherhood or motherhood includes accompaniment, but accompaniment does not include fatherhood or motherhood. They are two experiences that can go together, but are not coextensive. Nevertheless, some people prefer not to globalize spiritual paternity or maternity so as not to dilute and impoverish their meaning.

Although the Lord Jesus told his disciples to "call no one on earth your father; you have but one Father in heaven,"[17] his apostle Paul calls himself "the father" in relation to the communities he founded.[18] And it is most interesting to see that Paul,

13. Ibid., Prol. 21.
14. Ibid., 73.3.
15. Ibid., 2.2.
16. Ibid., 27.8.
17. Matt 23:9.
18. 1 Cor 4:15.

faithful to the word of the Lord, understands his paternity in a motherly way.[19]

Perhaps Paul's experience can help us understand better the deeper meaning of spiritual fatherhood, which is only understandable within the context of the church's motherhood over us all and, in a more personal way, in relation to the motherhood of the Spirit and of Mary. This is because the purpose of spiritual accompaniment and spiritual fatherhood consists in begetting Christ in the hearts of others and in helping Christians reach their full maturity in Christ, "the full stature of Christ."[20]

We should also notice that it is a question of *spiritual* maternity, that is, a motherhood that is a gift or charism of the Holy Spirit and that acts through the presence and power of the Spirit. This charism, when recognized and welcomed by the Christian community, becomes a service of ministry. It is precisely by the exercise of this service, with knowledge and prudence, that one best receives and grows in the Spirit's gift.

Mary of Nazareth, Mother of the Lord Jesus by the action and grace of the Holy Spirit, is also mother of the church and of each of her members. There is nothing better for all those who engage in the charismatic service of spiritual accompaniment, than to place themselves under the protection of Mary, so as to share in the grace of her motherhood.

19. See 1 Thess 2:7-8; Gal 4:19.
20. Eph 4:13.

Appendix I

THE SERVICE OF AUTHORITY

In his Rule for monks, our Father St. Benedict gives us two directories on the abbot. What he says there contains all we need to know. What could we add? A commentary? An update? An interpretation? A rereading? This last possibility is especially attractive.

There would be different ways to organize the rereading. Perhaps it could be according to the triple messianic mission of Christ as King, Prophet, and Priest; or something analogous to the functions of the Holy Spirit in the church as Soul, Communion, and Inspiration; or according to the service of the superior in its four dimensions of his or her relation to each person, to the community, to the order and to the church; or according to the five aspects of the abbot's service mentioned in our constitutions, those of father, teacher, shepherd, doctor, and administrator. We'll choose this last arrangement and use a classical literary genre not uncommon in the monastic past, namely that of "one-liners," or single sentences pregnant with practical wisdom and easy to remember.

1. *Father and Mother*

The first person to believe that you hold the place of Christ is you yourself, and that will help you act like him.

You are not Christ, but you hold his place; you don't take his place, but you represent him, above all, by what you do.

Whoever hears you hears him. Don't think that he does what you want or say, but rather you have to search for what he wants and make it known.

Your authority is a service to life, and this life needs your service more than your term of office.

The life you give and that you serve is not your own, but belongs to Someone else; to give life and to serve it, you must die to your own.

To serve life, you have to protect and promote it, motivate and orient it. Such service is both paternal and maternal. If you are not at the same time a father and a mother, you will be neither one nor the other.

The more mature you are, the better you can help others grow.

If you want to help others live, always think of what every person needs: meaning (a purposeful goal), belonging, and group identity.

To give life to others, you must be present, though not everywhere; and the degree of your presence is proportional to your moral authority.

Your authority is service, so the better you serve, the better will be your authority.

The life and legality of your authority come from above, but its guarantee is from below, in the quality of your service.

The credibility of your authority depends on (1) your capacity for listening, (2) your contact with others as they really are, (3) consistency between your words and your deeds, (4) your concentration on what is essential and important, and (5) the speed with which you fulfill your responsibilities.

The higher you go, the more you have to look at future horizons.

The four plagues afflicting monastic authority are *paternity* that abuses authority by confusing it with power, *fraternalism* that denies any hierarchy of services, *maternity* that needs to shelter or protect, and *infantilism* that looks for pleasant security by depending on others.

Stupid is the authority that takes jokes seriously and takes what is serious as a joke.

Authoritarianism is the first sign of an authority crisis.

Making your authority felt means you have a problem with obedience.

Your authority should never silence others, but rather make them think.

Many years of service can make you want to be served, but don't let that happen.

Keeping yourself in authority is to empty it of its meaning, to destroy its service.

Blessed are you if you contemplate the Lord and become radiant: the Lord will shed the light of his face upon yours for the glory of us all.

2. Model Teacher

To be a master you must first and always be a disciple of the only Master's Word.

If you want to be accepted as a master, always be a witness, not of perfection but of conversion.

If you live what you teach, don't be afraid to repeat what you say; it will never be the same.

Your teaching must be formational and transformational; only to inform is not to form.

As master, you must be able to articulate for others the essential values of their lives, their special goals.

The purpose of your talks can well be: (1) to *enthrall*, by captivating the attention of the listeners; (2) to *enlighten*, with the light of doctrine; (3) to *motivate*, by enkindling the emotions; and (4) to *convince*, in view of the decisions to be made.

You communicate well when you follow these principles: (1) *clarity*, by which they understand you; (2) *method*, in which you advance step by step; (3) *organic development*, producing harmony of content; and (4) *vivacity*, with examples from real life.

If you want to keep your listeners awake, be brief; if you want to be accepted, be yourself; if you want to bore them, be a know-it-all.

It is not a question of humor, but if you want to share what you know, entertain them and enjoy it.

The key to the art of formation is to know how to motivate, that is, how to wake them up, sustain their interest, and direct it.

To really motivate through your teaching demands your being natural, simple, and spontaneous, since nothing moves so much as certain ways of being and of self-expression.

Don't attempt to monopolize the teaching office, unless you want to keep the others in ignorance.

Blessed are you if you put a grain of salt in what you say, for everyone will find some sugar in what he or she feels.

3. Wise Shepherd

You are truly a shepherd the more you relate with each person as someone unique and unrepeatable.

If you listen with both your ear and your heart, you will know what the other is telling you and also what he or she is feeling.

Listen to those who speak to you; it is the simplest way of letting them exist.

All forms of shepherding are based on your capacity to identify with others and then differentiate yourself, to connect with them and then disconnect.

Your brother will listen to you when you get close to him, but not when he feels you are tracking him down.

All of us react toward others according to our past dealings with them.

Communication as a process is more emotional than intellectual; that is why it is so important to start with a welcome, then continue with another welcome and end the same way.

Ask the Lord for prudence; it will let you avoid the reefs of excess through inconsiderate precipitation and the pitfall of omission through neglectful inconstancy.

You will look for and find the common good when you can incorporate each one's special contribution into a higher harmony that integrates without destroying.

If you shepherd your flock so that the weak become strong, and don't neglect the strong because they make you feel weak, you are a good shepherd.

Life grows slowly; never despair.

Blessed are you if you experience everything as a grace, for you will be graced and a grace for everyone.

4. Merciful Doctor

If the miseries of your neighbor provoke your impatience and not your mercy, it is a sign that you have not yet accepted your own miseries.

The great majority of your present problems come from the past. What you tolerate now for lack of willpower will become a chronic evil: if you just let things happen so as not to cause waves, you will get a tsunami.

The best correction you can make is good guidance: the straight path is the one that is well marked.

A small dose of preventive medicine can save you from many infections and most incurable diseases.

Don't forget that a sense of humor is the pause that refreshes; when you are hot or tense, the remedy is a healing laugh.

Patience is almost all-powerful if it is a persevering peace and a dynamic passivity.

Blessed are you if you know how to distinguish a speck of dust from a high mountain, for you will avoid many useless anxieties.

5. Prudent Administrator

Always imitate your Lord and give priority to persons over things: first look at what each one is, then at what he or she does.

The personal responsibilities of your fellow workers are enriched by specifying their responsibilities.

Your projects receive their strength from sharing them beforehand with your fellow workers and your community, then appealing to their responsibility for carrying them out.

Projects are very important, but even more so are their beneficiaries and those who will implement them.

Long-term goals will let you set up programs to guide any six-year period with clarity and life.

Feedback and reviewing your work are good ways to improve what you have planned, said, and done.

Teamwork is a real help in increasing your capacity for being present to the community.

Respect the intermediate levels of administration and they will respect you.

The basic principles governing any good organization are:

— *Solidarity*: the solder that makes for bonding and reciprocal responsibility among the different officials and departments

— *Subsidiarity*: to protect the autonomy of decision and action of the different officials; what a subordinate superior can and should do should not be done by a higher superior

— *Participation*: the proper, proportionate interest of each official in the departments not falling under his or her direct responsibility; "invasion" is the corruption of participation, a "walled fortress" is its opposite

— *Intervention*: the possible operative or advisory presence on the part of a higher superior, so as to avoid conflicts or solve problems; "interventionism" is the corruption of intervention

— *Appeal*: the recourse made by a lower administrative level to the superior immediately above it so as to receive advice and assistance; jumping over the intermediate levels to "go to the top" is the corruption of any appeal

If the organization you have set up is functioning well, it will do so even in your absence.

The wisdom that comes from experience will let you be a good administrator and avoid these possible obstacles: (1) servile dependence on experts, (2) total trust in organizations, (3) waiting for science to confirm what common sense tells you is obvious.

It is best to entrust to specialists what is technically specialized and have it treated technically.

"Presidentialism" in an organization is to fill vacuums with a vacuum.

Blessed are you if you reflect before acting and laugh before reflecting, for you will avoid making many stupid mistakes.

And to conclude, we give the microphone to a great abbot of our order, Bernard of Clairvaux:

> Example given is indeed "a living and effectual word" (Heb 4:12), easily making what is said persuasive, by showing that what is commanded can be done. Therefore understand that on these two commands of word and example the whole of your duty and the security of your conscience depend. But if you are wise you will add a third, and that is devotion to prayer, so as to fulfill that threefold repetition of the command in the Gospel of St. John to feed the sheep. You will find that you can only fulfill the demands of the threefold sacrament if you feed your sheep by word, by example, and with the fruit of holy prayer. And so there are these three: Word, Example, and Prayer, but the greatest of these is prayer. For although, as I have said, the power of the voice is example, yet to both example and word, prayer gives grace and efficacy. (St. Bernard, *Letter* 201:3; in B. S. James, 259:3)

In other words, if we do not have time for prayer, we should resign in order to have it. We have to avoid confusing what is urgent and what is important. First things first!

Appendix II

WISE DECISIONS

We saw above, in chapter four, that in the spiritual tradition of the West, the word "discretion" means "discernment and moderation." We would like to present here two discreet ways of making decisions, that is, decisions that are correct and wise, thanks to a previous discernment of the situation.

Once again, we take Ignatius of Loyola as our master, together with his more outstanding followers. In Ignatian spirituality, discernment is a pedagogy of choosing, a process of liberation from liberty, so as to go beyond one's own judgments and self-will, thus peacefully finding and embracing the divine will.

We will try to be as schematic as possible and present two kinds of discerned decisions, the first one on a personal level, the second one consisting of options made by the community. Our interest here is completely practical. For pedagogical reasons, we offer a method with the following different steps: a prologue, the stages of the process, its fruits, and some pieces of advice.

MY PERSONAL DECISIONS

This first type of wise decisions consists in making them according to God's will in our daily lives.

Prologue

I put myself in the presence of Mary Immaculate, I let her look at me, and I ask the Holy Spirit to give me Mary's own *availability*. Like her, I must be ready to prefer and then embrace whatever is shown to be the will of God. This availability contains within itself several other attitudes or conditions that we can spell out as follows:

> Faith in seeing that God wants something from me in relation to the alternate possibilities at hand
>
> Being convinced that God will show his will through my reasoning process and my feelings
>
> Not looking for a divine confirmation of my own initial attractions
>
> Intending to embrace God's will whenever it is known, without previously laying down any conditions
>
> Becoming critically aware of the conditioning factors that influence me, chiefly:
>
> — The expectations of my social and cultural context: family, friends, study group or work group, and so forth
>
> — My initial, spontaneous motivation, conditioned by my search for pleasure and self-fulfillment
>
> — My self-justifying rationalization of these initial motives

Stages of the Process

> *Formulation* of the alternate options available, in a clear, precise way. If there are several alternatives, I try to put the possibilities in hierarchical order and only keep the two principal ones. If it is a question of only one option—such as offering to go on the foundation—I make it into two by putting it against its opposite; in this case it would be: I do not offer to go on the foundation.
>
> We should note that the matter of any discerned decision has to be something permitted, important, concrete, and doubtful. In one way or another it has to have a significant

role to play in our following of the Lord and our service to him.

Confrontation of the alternate options now formulated, permitting the reasons and feelings for and against each one to come to the surface and be expressed. It is better if we can do this in the course of more than just one day, so that we can become aware of a greater variety of our reactions. I can note these reasons and feelings, and arrange them in four columns, as follows:

I offer to go on the foundation		I do not offer to go on the foundation	
YES	NO	YES	NO

It is probable that some reasons and feelings can be put in two columns at the same time, that is, in favor of one alternate and against the other one. Actually this will not influence the final choice, since the importance of the reasons and feelings is more crucial than their mere number.

Weighing the importance of the reasons and feelings that have surfaced, in a climate of dependence on Mary. We now consider the inner movements in order to know where God's will is shown. The following two questions can help:

—Which reasons and feelings better reflect the Gospel and the New Man?

—Which reasons and feelings are less in accord with the Gospel and reflect the old man?

This weighing of our inner movements will gradually reject some of them and stress others, thus letting us come to a well-founded option. It is of the greatest importance at this stage to have the help of someone with experiential knowledge of making discerned decisions.

Decision, according to what has become clear as God's will through the reasons and feelings judged as more important in discerning where the new life of the Gospel is leading me.

Interior confirmation of the decision made. At this stage, it is best to renew our attitude of availability to the will of God in order to stress our inner freedom to embrace what he himself will confirm. Here are two methods of confirmation that are not mutually exclusive:

— Offer the decision to God and see if he confirms it with peace and consolation at the bottom of your heart.

— Offer the decision and see if God confirms it with silence. Then present the alternate option, which was not chosen, and see if there is any inner rejection, unpleasantness, or desolation.

This inner confirmation can be strengthened through an external confirmation, like that which could come from subsequent events or from a competent authority.

Fruits

Many of the fruits of prayer ripen in the process of discerned decisions. Among them are:

— Growth in love, since love is conformity of wills between God's and mine

— Sharing in Mary's availability and gift of self, which lets me become mother of Jesus, since I do the will of the Father

— A more fruitful participation in the history of salvation, since I have now freely decided on the salvation of my own history

Advice

Take all the time you need, because we know when prayerful discernment begins, but not when it will end.

Maintain your attitude of availability or, if necessary, renew it throughout the whole process. Experience teaches that the discernment process itself causes us to grow in availability.

A wise decision on very important matters, such as a change in one's state of life—becoming a priest or religious, getting married or remaining single—calls for a break from one's daily activities in order to withdraw and be alone with the Lord.

Prayerful discernment as we have presented it here presupposes alternate options that do not contradict the universal will of God. Cases of conscientious objection and contestation of human commands need special treatment.

In some instances, the decision we discern can go beyond what prudence or common sense dictates. The following of Christ and our service to him can sometimes imply such unsuspected risks, with the generosity that they require.

OUR COMMUNITY DECISIONS

This second type of discerned decision refers to community options according to God's will. A community united by particular bonds and common objectives is searching together for God's will in order to grow forward in it. Even though there are several ways to arrive at wise community decisions, all of them must include at least the following elements:

— *Matter* that is doubtful, but important

— *Availability* on the part of the individuals and the group

— *Prayer*, on both the personal and the communal level

— *Information* given and assimilated

— *Reasons* for and against

— *Decision* to be reached, preferably by consensus

— *Confirmation* of what is decided

The process we describe below is obviously just one among many possible ones. It is also obvious that some previous experience in coming to personally discerned decisions is an extremely important prerequisite. Since the process presented here is analogous to the one just described above, we will try to avoid unnecessary repetitions.

Prologue

We place ourselves in the presence of Mary Immaculate. We let her look at us and ask the Holy Spirit to give us Mary's own *availability*. After putting aside all self-interest, we are all prepared to search for the will of God and the common good, that is, what unites and guides the group in a common orientation.

• Stages of the Process

Information should be given. It has to be as complete as possible in whatever is related to the available options. It is important to take all the time needed to respond to the questions to be answered. The value of the opinions and evaluations will depend on the quality and adequate communication of the information.

The matter to be decided can be shared by the whole group, but it can also consist in decisions to be made by one of its members or in the necessary help needed for each member to come to a wise decision on his or her own situation.

Formulation of the alternate options available, in a clear, precise way. It is important that all members of the group understand univocally, that is, in the same way, what the alternate options imply.

Confrontation in prayerful solitude of the alternate options now formulated. This solitude should let the members *as-*

similate the information given, *study* the alternate possibilities, *distance* themselves from the group, and permit the reasons and feelings for and against each possibility to *come to the surface*.

Communication by each member, in prayerful solidarity with the group, of everything that came up during the personal confrontation. This communication should take place as follows:

— First, the communication of all the reasons *in favor*, the members speaking one by one, in order and without any interruptions

— A prudent *pause*, which can be for a couple of hours, or more

— All the reasons *against*, the members of the group speaking one by one, without any interruptions

This ordered, alternating procedure lets all the aspects of the matter be brought into the open. It frees everyone from their partial viewpoints in favor or against the proposal, and thus reduces defensive or aggressive reactions.

Of course, in order to achieve real solidarity and a full sharing, all involved must listen with their ears and their hearts, showing their respectful interest, understanding, and acceptance of their neighbor.

Weighing the importance of the reasons that have been communicated for and against the matter at hand, in a climate of prayerful solitude. This important stage, by taking into account the relative importance of each option in the light of prudence and the Gospel, will cause some reasons to be accepted and others to be put aside.

Sharing together prayerfully in an orderly way the results of the previous comparison between the pros, then the cons, of the proposed options. It is not only a question of presenting the reasons, but also of establishing their intrinsic worth.

The group will help each speaker to explain his or her motives.

If no decisive reasons are brought to light, for or against, the members of the group can once again clarify any doubts or feelings they might have, and go into solitude and reflect again on the importance of the reasons they have. It is also possible, according to circumstances, to take a straw vote in order to see where the thought of the group has arrived.

Final decision by a vote, preferably by group consensus. In case the opinions or reasons are equally divided between different possibilities, a compromise decision should be sought. It is always important to respect the minority by integrating its opinions.

Interior confirmation of the decision made by the group. God will make it felt by a joyful peace at the harmonious consensus achieved concerning the decision itself and its timing.

It is very probable that the group confirmation needs a further one on the part of competent authority and from future events. In case this later confirmation contradicts the decision reached through discernment, the conclusion is not necessarily that the decision was a mistake, but rather that it is not the right moment to act or that the decision is not applicable at this time.

Fruits

The following are the most typical fruits of prayerful group discernment:

— Continuing the work of Jesus as members of the church, because he came to do the will of his Father

— Growing in group cohesion and in communion with the body of the church

— Learning by experience that all the members working together are more intelligent than each one risking an adventure on one's own

Advice

If the group does not have one heart, a single "we" characterized by inner integration of its members and generous service to others beyond itself, there will not be a suitable agent for any wise decision.

In the same way, if the members do not "uncenter" themselves, so as to be centered on the Lord who is in their midst, any discerned option by the group will be impossible.

The stages of the process should let those who are strong serve the weaker members and help the latter become strong. If care is not taken to reduce the mechanisms of domination and submissiveness, there will not be any true consensus and concord.

A discerned decision by the group takes time, but much less time than decisions that are not discerned!

It is important that the group be open: that it feels itself to be part of the church community and of the larger human society in which it lives.

If group discernment concerns the signs of the times, the procedure described above could be enough, but the importance of such a topic calls for something special.

Appendix III

IGNATIAN RULES OF DISCERNMENT—I

RULES of St. Ignatius of Loyola (1st week):	INSTRUCTIONS OR DIRECTIVES		COMMENTS ON	
	GOOD SPIRITS:	EVIL SPIRITS:	THE ELEMENTS INVOLVED	THE PROCESSES INVOLVED
1:	Rouse and sting the conscience of those going from bad to worse	Propose apparent sensual pleasures to those going from bad to worse	Persons and their conflicting inner movements	Identification of the New Man and the old man
2:	Strengthen, console, and remove the obstacles for those doing better	Sadden and raise obstacles with fallacious reasoning against those doing better		
3:	GIVE CONSOLATION		Contrasting movements and thoughts	Identifying God's work and that of the evil one
4:		GIVE DESOLATION		
5:		Be firm and constant in not listening to the evil advice	Directory on Desolation	Growth in patience and humility by the road of desolation
6:		Intensely follow your former good resolutions		
7:		Remember that you have the grace to resist the enemy		
8:		Be patient and diligent in the good; soon you will be consoled		

#			Directory	
9:		Examine the causes: negligence, trials, self-knowledge	Directory on Desolation	Growth in patience and humility by the road of desolation
10:	Strengthen yourself for the next desolation		First Directory on Consolation	Pause on the journey to get strength and deepen humility
11:	Humble yourself, for you are very little without consoling grace	Strengthen yourself, since by using sufficient grace you can do much		
12:		The enemy is like a woman: weak in front of strength, but a tyrant if given her will, so reject his temptations at once		
13:		Like a false lover, he seeks to remain hidden and not be discovered, so be open with a spiritual accompanist	Directory on Temptation	Recognizing the enemy's tactics, so as to fight against him better
14:		Like a leader who attacks at the weakest point, so examine yourself on your virtues, vices, and personal shortcomings		

Appendix IV

IGNATIAN RULES OF DISCERNMENT—II

RULES of St. Ignatius of Loyola (2nd week):	INSTRUCTIONS OR DIRECTIVES		COMMENTS ON	
	ON GOOD SPIRITS	ON EVIL SPIRITS	THE ELEMENTS INVOLVED	THE PROCESSES INVOLVED
1:	Give happiness and joy, banishing sadness and disturbances	Fight against happiness and consolation with fallacious reasonings, subtleties, and deceptions	Contradictory spirits	Gateway to a second spiritual age
2:	God alone consoles *without* a previous cause		Directory on Consolation with or without a Cause	Maintenance of Peace in Time of Danger
3:	Both the good spirit and the evil one can console *with* a preceding cause, but for different purposes			
4:		It is a mark of the evil spirit to masquerade as an angel of light	Directory on Consolation in a Time of Ambiguity	

			Directory on Consolation in a Time of Ambiguity	Maintenance of Peace in Time of Danger
5:	See if the beginning and middle and end of one's thoughts and tendencies are wholly good; this is a sign of a good angel	See if the result of the thoughts and tendencies is evil, distracting, less good, or disquieting; this is a sign of an evil spirit		
6:		Gain experience by reviewing how the evil one gradually deceived us		
7:	In those who progress, the good spirit is like a drop of water penetrating a sponge, otherwise it is like water dropping on a stone	In those who progress, the evil spirit is like a drop of water falling on a stone, otherwise it is like water dropping onto a sponge		
8:	When consolation is without cause, one must examine the actual fact and its aftereffects; the latter may come from different spirits		Appendix to the Directory on Consolation with or without a Cause	

Appendix V

STAGES OF PERSONAL DEVELOPMENT

The stages and crises in the following tables are realities that can be *objectified*, but their most typical features cannot be. The maturing process depends, more than on life cycles, on: *authenticity*, which assumes personal responsibility for one's own life; *unconditionality*, which takes realities for what they are worth in themselves independently from one's own needs; *love*, which gives oneself over to others; *suffering* with its experiences of human limits; and the *presence of what is Absolute*.

Start of the Expansion Process (Age 0–40)
(The process of expanding human life consists in a process of differentiation or strengthening of the "conscious autonomous self." It implies self-adaptation to the family and to social reality, the creation of one's own existential space, affirmation, and creativity.)

Stages	Psychosocial Crises	Significant Relationships	Gifts to Conquer
Age 0–1	Trust or mistrust	Mother	Hope
First infancy Age 1–3	Autonomy or doubt	Parents	Security
Playmate Age 4–6	Initiative or guilt	Family and relatives	Achievements and resolutions
School years Age 6–12	Affirmation or inferiority	Neighbors and schoolmates	Competition

Stages	Psychosocial Crises	Significant Relationships	Gifts to Conquer
Adolescence Age 12–18	Identity or confusion	Friends, the group (team), idols, and heroes	Fidelity to self
Young adult Age 19–25	Intimacy-solidarity or isolation	Friends of both sexes, competitors, and coworkers	Love

Existential Crisis of One's Self-image (Age 20–25)
(Changes of social milieu and confrontation with what is different can often cause a crisis of the personal self-image. The person grows out of his or her ideal self and into the real self.)

Mature adult Age 25–60	Generativeness/creativity or unfruitfulness/ stagnation	Home, world of work, community, society	Good of one's neighbor

Crisis of Realism (Age 35–45)
(The world where we live our life project does not adapt itself to our plans and desires. The crisis of realism starts, lasting several years: "What do my projects mean?" The "whats" of my life become "for what.")

Crisis of One's Limits (Age 45–60)
(External reality has imposed itself upon our plans and desires, and there will be no other opportunity to achieve them. The crisis of limitation starts: no longer is it a question of creating reality, but of accepting it.)

Start of the Process of Introspection (Age 45–80)
(The psychological process of introversion is the growth from self-consciousness toward the true self, the individual's integrating center. This true self implies "letting oneself live," prescinding from one's social role, accepting and integrating one's negativity and inner contradictions.)

Ripe years Age 60–80	Integrity or despair	All humanity	Wisdom

SELECT BIBLIOGRAPHY

Accompaniment

AA., V.V. "Direction spirituelle." *Dictionnaire de Spiritualité*. Paris: Beauchesne (1957): t. III, cols. 1002–1215.

———. *La Paternité Spirituelle*. Séminaire pour maîtresses de novices cisterciennes. Laval, 10–15 (Septembre 1974) (Noncommercial).

Alurralde, P. "Spiritual Accompaniment." *A.I.M. English Language Bulletin* 87 (2006): 41–46.

Bamberger, J. E. "Spiritual accompaniment: observing love and its transformations." *Cistercian Studies* 37:4 (2002): 415–27.

Bonowitz, B. "*Fides ex Auditu*: The Novice Director Listens." *A.I.M. English Language Bulletin* 87 (2006): 37–41.

de Pinto, B. "Counseling and the art of spiritual direction." *Cistercian Studies* 21:2 (1986): 158–70.

Dubois, M. G. "L'accompagnement spirituel dans la tradition monastique hier et aujourd'hui." *Collectanea Cisterciensia* 51:1 (1989): 27–41.

Gratton, C. "Spiritual direction." Pp. 911–16 in *The New Dictionary of Catholic Spirituality*. Collegeville, MN: Liturgical Press, 1993.

Guy, J. C. "Sur la paternité spirituelle." *Collectanea Cisterciensia* 49:2 (1987): 186–89.

John of the Cross, Saint. *Collected Works of St. John of the Cross*. Translated by K. Kavanaugh and O. Rodriguez. Washington, DC: ICS Publications, 1964. (The quotations in the present book use this translation.)

Louf, A. "Governance and accompaniment in contemplative communities." *Cistercian Studies* 23:3 (1988): 193–210.

———. *La Grâce peut davantage. L'Accompagnement Spirituel*. Paris: Desclée de Brouwer, 1992.

———. "L'abbé et l'accompagnement spirituel." *Collectanea Cisterciensia* 62:3 (2000): 214–30.

———. "Un accompagnement spiritual concerté. Barsanuphe, Jean et Séridos." *Collectanea Cisterciensia* 66:1 (2004): 35–50.

May, G. *Care of Mind, Care of Spirit: A Psychiatrist Explores Spiritual Direction.* San Francisco: HarperCollins, 1992.

———. *Will and Spirit: A Contemplative Psychology.* San Francisco: HarperCollins, 1982.

Merton, T. *Spiritual Direction and Meditation.* Collegeville, MN: Liturgical Press, 1960.

———. "The Spiritual Father in the Desert Tradition." *Cistercian Studies* 3:1 (1968): 3–23.

Sellner, E. "Cassian and the Elders: formation and spiritual direction in the desert and today." *Cistercian Studies* 36:4 (2001): 417–35.

Sommerfeldt, J. R., ed. *Abba: Guides to Wholeness and Holiness, East and West.* Kalamazoo: Cistercian Publications, 1982.

Weakland, R. "The Abbot as Spiritual Father." *Cistercian Studies* 9:4 (1974): 231–38.

Discernment

AA., VV. "Discernement des esprits – Discrétion." *Dictionnaire de Spiritualité.* Paris: Beauchesne (1957): t. III, cols. 1222–1330.

Bertrand, D. "Bernard's Discernment: between the Desert Fathers and Ignatius." *Cistercian Studies* 36:4 (2001): 325–36.

Böckmann, A. "*Discretio* in Benedict's Rule and its tradition." *Tjurunga* 59 (2000): 14–26.

Buckley, M. "Discernment of Spirits." Pp. 274–81 in *The New Dictionary of Catholic Spirituality.* Collegeville, MN: Liturgical Press, 1993.

———. "Structure of Ignatian Rules of Discernment." *Theology Digest* 24:3 (1976): 280–85.

Cohelo, M. "Understanding Consolation and Desolation." *Review for Religious* 44:1 (1985): 61–77.

Dekkers, E. "*Discretio* dans Saint Benoît et Saint Grégoire." *Collectanea Cisterciensia* 46:2 (1984): 79–88.

de Vogüe, A. "Les trois critères de S. Benoît pour l'admission des novices." *Collectanea Cisterciensia* 40:2 (1978): 128–38; Spanish translation in *Cuadernos Monásticos* 14:54 (1980): 303–13.

———. "The Criteria for the Discernment of Vocations in the Ancient Monastic Tradition." *Cistercian Studies* 35:2 (2000): 144–60.

Dingjan, F. "Pour une révalorisation de la discrétion." *Collectanea Cisterciensia* 30:2 (1968): 147–59.

Emery, P. Y. "La consolation dans les 'Sermons pour l'année de saint Bernard.'" *Collectanea Cisterciensia* 52:3 (1990): 191–203.

Félix, P. "Les trois signes du discernement monastique." *Collectanea Cisterciensia* 54:2 (1994): 110–15.

Fiorito, M.A. *Buscar, Hallar la Voluntad de Dios*. Buenos Aires: Ed. Diego de Torres, 1989.

———. *Discernimiento y Lucha Espiritual*. Buenos Aires: Ed. Diego de Torres, 1985.

———. "La elección discreta según San Ignacio." *Boletín de Espiritualidad S.J.* 25 (1972): 3–66; 26 (1973): 3–67.

———. "Reglas de discernir de San Ignacio." *Boletín de Espiritualidad S.J.* 47 (1976): 22–42.

Gallagher, T. *The Discernment of Spirits*. New York: Crossroads, 2005.

Gil, D. *Discernimiento según San Ignacio*. Roma: Centrum Ignatianum Spiritualitatis, 1983.

Green, T. *Weeds among the Wheat. Discernment: Where Prayer and Action Meet*. Notre Dame: Ave Maria Press, 1984.

Ignatius of Loyola, Saint. *The Spiritual Exercises of St. Ignatius*. Translated by L. J. Puhl. Westminster: Newman Press, 1954. (The quotations in the present book use this translation.)

Kardong, T. *Benedict's Rule: A Translation and Commentary*. Collegeville, MN: Liturgical Press, 1996, esp. pp. 531–41 on RB 64. (Quotations from RB in the present book use this translation.)

Olivera, B. "Oración discerniente" y "Oración discreta." *Siguiendo a Jesús en María*. Buenos Aires: Soledad Mariana (2002): 2nd ed., 368–403.

Raabe, A. "Discernment of Spirits in the Prologue of the Rule of St. Benedict." *The American Benedictine Review* 23:4 (1972): 397–424.

Schindele, M. P. "Monastic Life according to St. Bernard." *Tjurunga* 52 (1997): 5–29.

Scholl, E. "The Mother of Virtues: *Discretio*." *Cistercian Studies* 36:3 (2001): 389–40.

Thomas, R. "La consolation chez saint Bernard." *Collectanea Cisterciensia* 53:2 (1991): 157–73; 53:3 (1991): 240–56.